Heaven
is
Our Final Home

Adrian + Kay

May your life be fully blessed from its pages!

MarJoe Davidson

No Rent   No Mortgage

MarJoe Davidson

Dedication

This book is dedicated to my mother, Mary Alice David-son, who was responsible for 'Heaven is Our Final Home' to have its life.

To my beautiful baby sister, Carol, fifty-nine years old, who was responsible for the final chapter of this book.

To my wonderful brother James, who realized that family, needed to be together, and he and Pat made the decision that they would move from Texas City, Texas to Lopez Island, Washington so the three of us could spend the rest of our senior years together.

To my dear sister, Pat, who shared with me the message she received of greater things to come. This message was given to Pat in God's own voice.

To my spouse, Natalie, who after being together for 25 years, we were finally able to be married on our anniversary August 13, 2013, in our garden, on Lopez Island. She has been instrumental in trying to keep me on track to get this book, to Bookmasters, so it could go to print. She listened to my vision of the book cover and came up with a beautiful book cover concept. Thank you, Natalie, for all you do and have done to get this book out of my hands and into the hands of the readers.

Foreword

As I started writing this book I had no idea how I was going to explain the five and one-half hour journey into Heaven that Pat, Carol, and I took with mother. So I found myself writing chapters 1 through 11 and chapters 13 through 19. Chapter 12 was to be about three sisters' account of this majestic experience and a brother who testified to its validity.

At the time I lived in Marblemount, Washington located at the foot of the Cascade Mountains. Across the road from my house was a small roadside chapel, with seating for about eight people. It was a place where I would go daily to relax and think about what I wanted to write that day.

After nine months of writing it was now time for chapter 12. As per my ritual, so to speak, I approached the little church. I found myself asking, "God, how and what am I going to write so people will understand your mighty work. How can I put it into words, so those reading this book, will not be confused, but let this experience flow easily and engulf each one into this miracle?"

As I stepped onto the front porch of the little chapel two women came out of the doorway.

One of the women said, "This is a beautiful little church." I answered, "Yes it is. I come here every day to sit and mediate before I continue writing on my book." "What is it about," she asked. I gave them a summary about the book. Then one of the women said, "I just love Revelation 21:1-4. Heaven is a wonderful place. Where we will all be happy, no crying, sorrow or pain.

They left and I went inside to meditate. There was a bible on a stand in the front of the church. I got up and went over and opened the book to Rev. 21:1-4. The verses were as the woman had said. Then I read verse 5. All things new. And he said to me "Write for what I say is Trustworthy and True." It was then I knew in my heart and soul that God had answered my question. "God how will I make Chapter 12 flow for the readers to understand?" I knew that I had no worries about this, as God would put into my heart what to write.

I walked back to the house. Natalie, my life partner, was sitting in the living room. "Natalie, I am ready to write chapter 12." I told her.

I sat down at the computer and said, "God, I am ready," and with no hesitation I, no God, through me, began writing chapter 12 and I wrote throughout the day and by early morning the next day the chapter was finished. I got up from the computer and walked to the bedroom climbed into the bed, and I began to cry. Natalie woke up and asked, "What's wrong?" I answered, "The book is finished."

Acknowledgments

Liz Lafferty; Thank you so much for being available to help me put these pages in the order they needed to go. To take the time to do a lot of the editing of the new pages added for the Final Chapter. A person sometimes comes into your life and at first is not revealed just why. We met, became friends, and then you learned that I was writing a book. You let me know that maybe you could help me. Boy, Liz did you ever help me with getting it ready for print. You put me on a schedule of meeting with you once a week for about two months and giving me instruction as to what you wanted from me the next time we were to meet. You kept me writing and I kept you editing. Thank you so much Liz, not only do I have the book ready for print but I have you as a friend.

To my spouse and my family; Thank you for encouraging me to do the best I could to let the world know of this place called Heaven. It is indeed our final home.

I thank the many people who have crossed my path to answer the questions that I and others have had after completing my original book.

John 14:2 In my Father's house are many mansions: if it were not so I would have told you that. I go to prepare a place for you.

Contents

Introduction

I am MarJoe Davidson and am writing this book as Mary Joe, about the extraordinary life of my mother, Mary Alice Davidson. This vibrant, compelling woman was diagnosed to have lung cancer and twelve tumors on her brain. This book is an account of the final four months that my sisters, brother and I had with this most precious and caring woman that we called 'Mother.'

Mary Alice Petray was born in London, Arkansas on August 13, 1912. She was the third born of eight children to Joseph Calvin and Annie Hines Petray. Her father owned a general store and also trapped for furs. Her mother was a housewife and kept quite busy looking after the children. Mother grew up in a loving, close-knit family who took care of each other. It was the time of the Great Depression and all money was needed to keep the family fed, clothed and sheltered. As a teen-ager, Mother worked in the local bakery and would bring home day-old bread for the family. On payday she would give her paycheck to her mother. To supplement the family's income she also worked in the cotton fields picking cotton, and this paycheck, too, went into the family coffers. Despite her various jobs, Mother continued her schooling while many of her friends had to drop out to help support their families. She had some wonderful memories of those days and shared them with me on many occasions. Mother would get a twinkle in her eyes when she talked about playing basketball for the Malvern High School team. At the time she was five-feet-one inches tall and weighed one hundred pounds. Listening to her reminisce about the games I could just envision this little ball of pure energy ricocheting around the court.

On August 13, 1936, Mother married James Joseph Davidson, it was her twenty-fourth birthday. James was born July 28, 1910 in Russellville, Arkansas. He was the first born of four children to James Joseph and Johnnie Faust Davidson. My mother, Mary Alice, and father, James Joseph had four children. Mary Joe, James David, Patricia Ann and Carol Jean. I was born in Missouri; my brother, James and sister, Patricia were born in Arkansas; and my youngest sister, Carol, was born in Washington State.

In the summer of 1944, my father left Little Rock, Arkansas to work at the Hanford Engineer Works Plant in Washington State. We stayed behind and he sent for us in the fall. Mother, with three children under the age of seven and a fourth child expected in the spring, boarded a train to travel half-way across the United States. It was the height of World War II and the trains were full of soldiers who had returned to the United States from their duty overseas or were going to their next assigned military base. I can remember how helpful and protective several of the soldiers were toward my mother and her little brood. My dad met us at the train station in Sunnyside, Washington and, as I looked back at the train, some of the soldiers that had traveled the many hundreds of miles with us were standing there smiling. It was if they were saying, "We got your little family to you, James.

"Dad had rented a house in Richland for us. Carol Jean was born a few months after we arrived.

As Dad worked for the government, it took care of many of our needs. Our medical, dental and rent costs were very low. Our three bedroom duplex was quite spacious and we had a lot of freedom: we could pick cherries, plums, apples and asparagus on government land. The fruits were amazingly big. Mother did a lot of canning and baking from the fruits and vegetables that we were able to pick for free. 'Free' little did we know how much that would cost us later in all our lives? The base did have restrictions though; we never saw where Dad worked. He was a civilian employee at Hanford working for the United States government. Dad was very secretive; he never talked about what he did inside the plant. Mother must have sensed the dangers associated with 'The Plant.' She was very insistent that we never go near Dad's lunch pail, I remember it was always kept out of our reach. As a child I never understood about the lunch pail, but Dad had his reasons and Mother upheld his wishes. Years later, we learned that he worked in the building where the Atomic Bomb was assembled. After the war Dad became a patrolman guarding the perimeters of the Hanford Plant. It remained off limits to all but those who worked there.

I recall that there were times the town's people were told to stay indoors because the government was spraying for insects. At the time we didn't question it, but forty years later we found out the spraying was, in reality, radiation being emitted into the atmosphere. The number of total releases from 1943 through 1950 was 128 times. These releases were equivalent to 530,000 curies of radiation. By way of comparison, at Three Mile Island, the release was 15 curies and the world was concerned! We ate the food and drank the milk and lived our lives not knowing what the United States government, my country, was exposing us to.

We left Richland, Washington in June 18, 1949 and have learned of the consequences of having lived there. I received a phone call from Mother sometime in December, 1988. She asked me if I had seen or heard the program on 'Good Morning America' that day. I told her that I hadn't seen the program and why was she wanting to know. She informed me that it had something to do with Hanford, Washington, but that she tuned in at the end of the show so she missed the contents of the program. Mother seemed concerned about what she might have missed but I didn't think at the time that it was something of importance, so I forgot it. Later, I found out that

Mother then called Pat to see if she had seen the show. Pat's response was the same as mine. She also called Carol and with that call she found out the terrible news about the releases of radiation on her and her family during the time we lived in Richland, Washington. Carol immediately called the television station to inquire about the program on 'Good Morning America.' The station told her what it was about and gave her a phone number to call in Washington, D.C. for further information. She called and was given a phone number for the Center for Disease Control in Atlanta, Georgia. She made the call and what she found out would change my thinking about this country.

I love my country and would have given my life in defending its borders. But now I have these questions. Why did my country do this to me and my family? Why didn't my country love us and the thousands of people in the Hanford area? The United States government let us live there and released radiation on us, then let thousands of people leave the area after the War without telling anyone what they had done.

The information that I received also made me more aware of my own health and left me wondering about the damage the radiation might have had on me. I had two miscarriages during my childbearing years and even my mother and two sisters had miscarriages. Now maybe some questions can be answered. Radiation, what did it do to my body and to the bodies of each member of my family? Why did the government wait to let us know? I found out later that many people who lived in the Hanford area also began asking questions as to why there were more incidents of cancer in people who lived there during the 1940s. The United States government was ordered to open the Hanford files, and we learned our fate. Now the government was forced to tell the world what they did to their own people!

When we first heard the report about the radiation releases, Mother's response was, "Why? Oh, why, did they let me keep my little children out there?" That was about all I ever heard my mother say about this devastating news.

Shortly thereafter, my mother, who had never been seriously sick a day in her life, suffered what was diagnosed as a mild stroke. Nine months later, on October 3, 1989, she was diagnosed with cancer. Mother decided to agree to the treatments prescribed by her physicians. "If there is no change after the chemotherapy and radiation treatments, I will not continue with further treatments," she told her doctors.

The first few treatments of radiation of the head took a toll on her body and her health quickly declined. She began to refuse to eat. She lost strength in her legs and was unable to walk without the use of a walker or, only, with our help. She needed help taking a bath and getting dressed. After her first infusion of chemotherapy complications arose. She developed pneumonia and became incontinent. She was given insulin due to a chemical imbalance of a hormone.

We respectfully carried out Mother's wish and eventually brought her to my sister, Carol's, home to live out her last days with dignity. Her loved ones could care for her with help from a local hospice program, and with additional support from the American Cancer Society.

While I'm no expert on death, the hospice program or life after death, I do feel qualified to write about what we experienced. My sister and I were privileged to witness a remarkable spiritual experience of white light, rays of gold and silver, while Mother's spirit interacted with each of us for over five and one half hours. This was Mother's last gift to us and it left an impression on me that will last for the rest of my life. This experience validated for me that there is life after death. . .the 'spirit.'

Our experience caring for Mother is also worth sharing because, as the population grow older and health care expenses continue to rise, it is a fact that more Americans will be caring for their loved ones in a home setting, including caring for those who are terminally ill.

The aim of this book is to familiarize those persons who, may one day, become a care giver for a terminally ill person, with how a hospice program works, how to become involved with services that are available, how to interact with family and support personnel, and how my family viewed their part in this incredible transition between life and death.

No words could begin to express the love I hold for my mother and I know my sisters and brother had the same feeling for her. In waiting for death, I want to give an account of feeling and emotions that I, and yes, we, the family had toward this wonderful soul.

Living with death is an everyday process until that person dies. The family has to create as normal a life as possible and yet be available to care for this person.

This was a commitment we made to our dying mother. Her last gift of love to us was filled with many miracles, as we shared a wonderful life after death experience on the Other Side with her. It was after the spiritual experience and the miracle that took place the night before Mother passed on, that we learned we had lived with and in the presence of an Angel in disguise.

On January 19, 1990 Mother passed away at the home of my sister with children, granddaughter, great-granddaughter and her sister at her side.

This book is a tribute to the memory of Mary Alice Davidson, a remarkable woman in her life-time, and to that Higher Being that we know, without a doubt, allows her to live on
. . . IN THE SPIRIT . . .

1

The Call

Mother was admitted to the hospital on October 3, 1989. Carol had called me at work, "Mary Joe, Mother has just had an x-ray and Mary there is a spot." I could not even remember Carol's last words past the word spot. I was sick inside; something like that wrong with my mother? Never! Then as I drifted back I could hear Carol's voice, "Mary Joe are you there? Mary..."

"Yes, Carol, I'm here. Oh, Carol I can't believe it."

"Neither can I Mary," she sobbed. "The Doctor wants to know when Mother last had a chest x-ray. I can't remember."

I could feel the adrenalin begin to flow as I responded, "Carol, Mother had an x-ray when she was in General Hospital back in December, 1988, when she had her stroke. Call them right now and get those films. They have to release them to you."

Carol answered with vigor, "Mary Joe, that's right. I'll call them right now."

She made the call and was told she could pick up the x-rays the next morning.

I arrived at Northwest Medical Hospital later that afternoon after work. Mother informed me immediately that Dr. Thomas had called in another doctor, Dr. Jones, an oncologist, for consultation. Mother had been complaining of dizziness and nausea and now, with a spot on her lung, Dr. Thomas wanted her to have the best medical advice that was available.

More in-depth tests were to be performed the next morning, which would entail another scan of the chest and a C.A.T. scan of the head. Since Carol was going to pick up the x-rays the next day from General Hospital I spent the night with Mother. The x-ray technician arrived early that morning to take Mother for her test.

I sat and waited for Carol to get there. I thought back to those words that she had spoken less than twenty-four hours ago, spot on her lungs. These words and ones I would hear in a few hours would change my life forever. Carol arrived with a brown folder under her arms, jubilant that she had obtained the all important x-rays. She took the films from their folder.

"Mary Joe, let's take a look at them and see if we can see anything," she said, as she put the first x-ray, of Mothers lungs, against the window, letting the sunlight filter through to give us a clear view. "Do you see anything, Mary Joe?"

"Well I'm no doctor, but I believe that this area looks like a spot or something different." I pointed to the area.

"Mary, I believe you're right."

We then proceeded to look at the other head x-rays; I couldn't see anything in the remaining x-rays but, as I stated, I was no doctor.

"Mary Joe, was Mother nervous when she went down for her test?"

"I think she was, Carol, but you know Mother, we would be the last to know."

We sat together for a while and talked about the discovery that we felt we had made. Our mother had a spot on her lungs in December 1988. I can't believe that Dr. Matson had not checked her further, during the nine months that we had her into his office or the phone calls that were made about her symptoms and declining condition. I will never understand this doctor's lack of concern and his indifference toward his patient, my mother.

"Mary Joe, let's take the x-rays down to the radiologist."

We had met Dr. Nancy Allison the day before when she showed us Mother's chest x-ray. We stood at the elevator and we both agreed that we wanted to show Dr. Allison where we thought there was a spot; I suppose to see if we were right.

The elevator door opened and out stepped Dr. Thomas. Excitedly we told him that we had the x-rays from General Hospital and we were on our way down to give them to Dr. Allison.

He took several steps closer toward me to be clear of the elevator. "It's worse than we thought," he stated as he looked at me, then to Carol.

'What is this man saying?' I thought; 'what could be worse than a spot on my mother's lungs?'

"Would you rather I tell you both out here or do you want to go to your mother's room and I will tell all of you at the same time."

"Tell us here," we both responded.

Then his words came at me like a knife cutting into my heart and I could feel my legs beginning to buckle under me.

"Your mother not only has a tumor on her lungs, but she has twelve tumors in her head."

This doctor was telling me that the person who I knew as my mother, my traveling companion, my dear friend and often my counselor had twelve tumors in her head and by the next day we would know that they were cancerous. I wanted to cry, scream and run as if to leave this terrible news behind me. This couldn't be happening. Mother, Mother, my poor mother now we must let you know! We needed time to get our composure before we went into Mother's room.

As Mother listened to the news, my heart was breaking, looking at this five-foot one inch tall, gray haired woman I had known for fifty-two years, sitting there on the edge of the bed, taking this devastating news. Mother didn't cry, for this was not what she generally did in the presence of her children, although

I have seen her cry on several occasions. This warm, considerate and loving person who always thought of her fellow person was now thinking about her two daughters standing there. She would have to be strong for her daughters. Oh Mother, Oh Mother.

The doctor left the room. Mother turned to me, "Mary, we must call the family."

'Call family,' I thought; 'I can't even talk for fear that I will start crying in front of Mother.'

"Carol get my address book out of my purse," she stated.

So started the calls. The first two went out to Pat and James.

"Pat, its Mary Joe."

"Yes, Mary, I've been waiting to hear from you. I couldn't sleep at all last night. I cried a lot, and I'm still crying off and on. Do you know anything about the C.A.T. Scan Mamma had this morning?"

"Yes, Pat, the news is not good."

"Mary Joe, oh god, Mary what do you mean," her voice was breaking and she began to sob.

"Pat, Mother has got..." the words were stuck in my throat.

Carol took the phone out of my hand and said, "Pat, Mom has twelve tumors in her head."

Pat became hysterical, crying uncontrollably but managed to keep talking, "Carol, how is Mamma right now; I, uh, I mean how did she take the news. Carol, oh Carol, my precious mamma."

Jack, Pat's husband was home so we felt better knowing that Pat would not be there by herself after we hung up. The next call went to James.

"James, we have the report from this morning's test." I explained to him all that we had been told.

James was silent for a long time. 'Uh, uh, uh.' He responded, "Mary Joe tell Mom I will be over this afternoon." James was not one to say much when around the family. I sometime wondered about this man, my brother, who had in the past been a vice president for one of the largest trucking companies in the U.S. He is outgoing, aggressive and well-liked by all who know him. He started working as a dock worker at eighteen years old and advanced himself to a management position in the trucking industry. He was very personable, but around our family he never talked much about his feeling.

There were five more calls to make to Pauline, Joan, Aline, Cecil and Junior, Mother's sisters and brothers. Mother talked to each one after we broke the news of her diagnosed cancer. This very strong and independent woman had inherited the matriarch position in the family, passed on by her mother Annie Hines. She was loved and highly respected by all members of her family, who telephoned her frequently. It was if all would think that 'I talked to Mary. She is my rock.'

I took the phone from Mother when she finished talking to Junior. "Junior, it's Mary Joe."

His words were broken and he began to cry. "Mary Joe, I can't believe that this has happened to Mary Alice. I always felt that she would out live us all."

"I know Junior I always thought that, too. We are going to be talking to the oncologist, Doctor Jones later today about the choice of treatments."

"Mary Joe, please keep us informed."

"I will," I said as I hung up the phone.

The family was now aware of the period of beginning our journey to the end.

The nurse came into the room to give Mother a sedative to help her rest through the evening; the doctor felt she would need something after hearing the news. Mother dozed off to sleep.

The phone rang. "Hello," I answered.

"Mary Joe, this is Pat. I called Southwest Airlines and I'm booked to arrive at Dallas Love Field tomorrow night at nine o'clock. Could someone pick me up at the airport? There's no way I can stay down here. I've been crying ever since I hung up the phone talking to you all and to Mamma. I want to be with Mamma; I want to be able to see her and to put my arms around her and to hold her. Mary I've been praying that she will be okay and that the treatments help her. Oh, Mary Joe, I don't know what I will do if I lose my mamma."

Tears began to stream down my face as Pat was talking, no truer words were ever spoken. What will I do without her? Later James came to the hospital; Carol and I left the room so James could be alone with Mother. We returned to her room thirty minutes later and as we walked back into the room we could hear Mother telling James, "Don't cry son, everything will work out."

I went over the events of the day and let him know that Pat was due to arrive at the airport the next night and asked him if he could pick her up. He said that there would be no problem meeting Pat as he needed to work late the next day and would be over near Love Field at that time anyway.

Dr. Jones, the oncologist, walked into the room just as Carol and James were getting ready to leave. I was glad that he had caught us all there with Mother as it gave him an opportunity to tell all of us what he was going to do the next day. The procedure he explained was a bronchoscopy. He would insert a scope through Mother's mouth into her throat and down into the bronchial tubes to look at and take pictures of the spot that showed up on the chest x-ray. He told her that he wanted her to take the sleeping pill that he had prescribed, as she would need to get a full night's sleep. He also told her he was starting her on a medication (Decadron) to help reduce pressure in her head due to the tumors located there. I guess that could be the reason that Mother had experienced dizzy-headedness all this time. At this time, he said the medication would be given by intravenous push, directly into the veins. Also since Mother was still nauseated, Phenergan IV was ordered to be given. She would be getting Reglan by intravenous piggyback for her nausea and for reducing any gastric secretions that might cause discomfort.

Dr. Jones left the room. Our conversation was limited to small talk, as I found it hard not to get choked up when I opened up my mouth. James and Carol finally left. I stayed with Mother again that night as I knew that Pat would want to stay with her Thursday night when she arrived from Texas City.

Mother took her sleeping pill and within thirty minutes she had drifted off into a peaceful sleep. I sank back into the comfortable easy chair and cried softly thinking about the day, and before long I was myself free of all that had gone on that day.

Throughout the night I woke up every time Mother turned in the bed, just as I remembered doing with my two babies' years ago. I was her child and also mother to my mother.

I awoke Thursday around five thirty a.m. and I sat there crying and holding Mother's hand, reliving all that had gone on the day before. Suddenly, I felt her hand gently come across the top of my hand.

"Mary Joe, what's wrong?" she spoke as she moved to a sitting position on the side of the bed.

Before I knew what I was saying I blurted out, "Mother I'm so angry with you; you led us to believe you would always be okay."

She looked at me with those wonderful caring eyes and responded, "Mary Joe, I'm a human being. I'm just like you. I'm not immortal and I'm so sorry if I've ever led you, any of you, to think that way."

I fell on my knees, to the floor, in front of her and she held my head to her breast and we cried.

2

The Diagnosis

Mother had talked to several of her friends at the Senior Citizen high-rise where she lived. They received the news with absolute shock and disbelief. Mother was loved by many of the residents that lived there as she had touched many of their lives. "Are you going to return to your apartment Mary Dee?" was the question that most of them asked after she told them of her disease.

"Sure I am; don't write me off as dead yet," was Mother's reply.

She hung up the phone from her last call, turned to me and looked straight into my eyes and said, "Mary Joe, I believe I will beat this. I will give it my best shot, I know that much."

I remember her words as clear and to the point but in her eyes the question was there: Mary Joe will I really make it? I remained silent. My answer was not in words but my eyes and face must have shown my innermost feelings. I hope so Mom, but the odds are not good. If only it was just the lung cancer. Maybe you would have a better chance. Twelve tumors in the brain tips the scales in the other direction.

Dr. Jones sat down with Carol and me and told us the results of the bronchoscopy. The tumor located at the Y of the bronchial tubes was malignant. The position of the tumor proved to be inoperable. The doctor told Mother the test results and discussed the treatments with her. "I cannot promise anything Mary Alice, but I do know that chemotherapy has proven to be good treatment when the small oak leaf cancer is involved and that is what you have. Also it is effective when the tumor is rapidly growing as in your case. The cells are more sensitive to the chemotherapeutic agents when they are undergoing division. This would be my choice of treatment for your lungs but for the tumors located in the brain I would recommend radiation treatments for them."

It was hard to concentrate on what he was saying, chemotherapy and radiation, these words have been so familiar in my nursing career but now they were words that seemed so foreign. The description of the treatments would be repeated by Dr. Jones once more when all four of Mother's children would be by her side.

The day was a long one, from the time of receiving the news, to making the phone calls to family and friends and letting them know the latest findings. Pat would be here today and I knew she would be busy getting her family prepared for her time away from home so I decided that it would be better to tell Pat the results of the bronchoscopy when she arrived. Anyway what could she do except cry and be more upset?

James brought Pat to the hospital where Carol and I met them outside of the Emergency Room entrance. We all held on to each other and cried for several minutes. I filled Pat in on everything that had transpired that day. As I spoke the words came between sobs.

"Oh, Mary Joe, I am so mad at that doctor that wouldn't listen to you or Carol."

"I know, Pat," I replied as I thought back to nine months ago when all of this began.

****

I remembered when Mother called my office at two o'clock on December 27, 1988. "Chris, is that you? Can I speak to Mary Joe?"

Chris buzzed me, "Mary Joe it's your mother calling."

"Hi, Mother, how are you doing today?"

"Not so good," was her reply. Then she proceeded to tell me that she had an appointment to see Dr. Waters the next day. Her voice was weak and her speech slurred. This was not like Mother at all. I talked to her a while longer, and then hung up.

Chris was standing in the doorway. "Mary Joe, what's wrong with Mary, she didn't sound like herself."

"I don't know Chris, but I'm going to call Carol to see if she has talked to Mother today."

Carol picked up the phone on the second ring.

"Carol, Mary Joe here. I just hung up from talking to Mother and she tells me you are taking her to see the doctor tomorrow."

"Yea, that's right she's not feeling very peppy."

"Carol, I believe that Mother may be having a stroke or getting ready to have one. Her voice was very slurred and she appeared to be having trouble forming sentences coherently. She may need to see the doctor now or to be taken to the hospital emergency room immediately."

"I'll call Mother as soon as I hang up and I'll also call Dr. Waters," she replied. "I'll call you back as soon as I talk to them, Mary Joe."

It seemed like forever before Carol called me back, but in reality only five minutes had passed by. "Mary Joe, I'm taking Mother to General Hospital Emergency Room. You were right, she doesn't sound like herself. Dr. Waters told me to get her right over to the hospital. Mother says she is not going to go but I told her I would bring Dwight (Carol's husband) to carry her down the stairs if he had to. She agreed to go when I told her, but she was not very happy that I was making her do this."

"I'll meet you at the hospital, Carol. I'm leaving now."

"I was so glad that my friend, Natalie, happened to be at the office. I asked her if she would to drive me to the hospital. This was the first of many times that she wound up supporting me and my family through the course of Mother's illness.

Carol was in the waiting room of the emergency room when I arrived. "Mary Joe, Mother is in with the doctor now. I'm so glad that she called you, and that you were able to detect something was wrong."

Mother mentioned that she was dizzy-headed and nauseated. She was admitted into the hospital that evening.

The next day was the beginning of tests to verify just what had happened to Mother. I knew without a doubt that it was going to be hard trying to keep her in the hospital for any length of time as she was never sick and she was always on the go.

Some of the tests were chest x-rays, C.A.T. scan of head, and carotid scanning as well as blood work up. The report from the chest x-ray and the C.A.T. scan of the head was reported to us by Dr. Matson as being negative, in other words there was nothing found in these areas.

The doctor stated that the carotid scanning showed buildup of plaque in the veins of the neck. This was probably the cause of her attack. Mother remained in the hospital and after three days she was discharged to go home with medications that Dr. Matson prescribed for her.

Carol usually took Mother back to the doctor's office for her scheduled appointments and would let the doctor know that Mother did not seem to be improving. Dr. Matson at that point changed her medication and sent her home to, experiment, in other words try the new drugs. Several follow up phone calls were made to Dr. Matson that Mother was having problems. Carol had requested on different occasions to have some other test run, but this seemed to fall on the doctor's deaf ears.

Mother, over the next nine months, carried on with her daily routine but not with as much vim and vigor as she had in the past.

Mother had an appointment, September 29, to see Dr. Matson and Carol asked me if I could take Mother as she was busy that day. I didn't have a class that day at the Nursing School, so I agreed to take Mother. I was rather glad that I was going as I wanted to talk to the doctor face to face. Mother was still complaining of dizzy-headedness and nausea during the past nine months, and over a six month period she had lost twenty pounds, from one hundred and thirty-four pounds to one hundred and fourteen pounds. I was concerned!!

Mother and I arrived at the doctor's office and had to wait only a few minutes. Dr. Matson did the basic examination, blood pressure, temperature, respiration, pulse rate and weight. Mother didn't talk to doctors very much. I guess it was due to the fact that she was never ill. She never developed that bond that comes with a patient/doctor relationship. I explained to the doctor all the symptoms and complaints that Mother was having.

"Dr. Matson, Mother has lost quite a bit of weight and still is nauseated and dizzy-headed. Don't you think that you could put her in the hospital and run some tests to see what is causing this?" I begged.

"No, I do not think that would be necessary. I believe that she is experiencing an inner ear infection and that is causing her to be nauseated and dizzy-headed. I will give you several names of ear doctors. You may choose which one you want to take her to."

"But, Doctor, I think..."

"Look I'm going to take your mother off all the medication and put her on this one. If, after she sees the ear specialist she is not any better, we will take it from there."

I took Mother home and went over to the pharmacy to have the prescription filled. I made sure that Mother knew the directions for taking the new medication. I gave her one pill then I headed home.

Shortly after I got home, the phone rang. "Hello."

"Hi, Mary Joe this is Carol. What did the doctor say about Mom?"

It had been less than an hour since I left Mother and I figured that Carol would have called Mother to find out the report, but I guess she wanted to hear it from me first. I proceeded to give Carol the scoop on what Dr. Matson said.

"Ear infection my ass," Carol replied. "Mary Joe, I just talked to Mom. She is still nauseated and now she is vomiting. I told her not to take any more of those pills and I also called Dr. Matson to inform him of her symptoms. Mary Joe, I'm going to take Mom to another doctor the first of the week."

****

As I drifted back, to the present, I felt Pat's arm tighten around my shoulder and I realized that we four Pat, Carol, James and I were standing outside the hospital crying and huddled together each one I imagine wondering; 'Why? Oh why did this cancer have nine months to grow? Oh. Oh. So sad. So sad.'

Pat wanted to know why Carol and I had left Mother's room.

"Pat, Mother was getting tired of us hovering over her since Tuesday. She wanted a little time to herself," I answered.

I let myself contemplate, as the four of us walked back to Mother's room. Mother loved her family and most times was the one responsible for the family get-togethers, but she also liked her privacy and her independence. She would lose all this, during the next four months, to her children and to those in the medical field.

Pat walked into Mother's room and quickly moved to the bed falling into Mother's waiting arms. They were oblivious to all that was around them for that moment. Pat cried uncontrollably and Mother comforted her with her soft and loving words. Pat stayed the night; she told me later that she and Mother talked far into the wee hours of the morning.

I was up early Friday morning as I wanted to get an estimate to remodel a room. Thursday morning the social worker at the hospital talked to Mother about alternatives available if she began to need constant care. She gave her several options at that time. They agreed that the two best options are: She could return to her apartment and her children could take turns staying with her, or she could move in with one of her children.

I had a two car garage that had been converted into a finished room. It had a bathroom and shower installed. Mother and I had talked about this as being a very workable solution. I knew that this would happen only if Mother was unable to remain at her apartment.

I called my good friend Paul, who was in construction, to come by and go over some changes to the room and give an estimate for what it would cost. We had worked together in construction for Raldon Homes as superintendents. If I had had the time I could have done the work myself but there would be no time allowed for me to even think about it. I knew I could depend on Paul if I had to get the room ready quickly.

I told Paul, "Mother loves the outdoors, I want to install a window that overlooks the back yard and put in a few cabinets and make a small kitchenette with a small bedroom off the large room. I want her to be able to have family members over to visit at her little apartment without having to come through my part of the house if they don't want to."

Paul let me know that he could do the work within a week if I needed to get it done. Mother wanted to remain independent and I wanted her to be able to for as long as she could. I knew that I would be only a door away from her, and my plans were to install a direct intercom from her room to my bedroom so if she needed me through the night she could call for me. Then, I would also be able to monitor her throughout the day as her illness progressed. But, right now I was working with a hypothetical situation. Mother's wishes at this point were to return to her apartment, that she had lived in for the past ten years and to be close to her friends.

3

The Journey Begins

Dr. Jones came into the room on Friday afternoon, October 6. Pat, Carol, James and I were with Mother and we knew that he would want to explain the treatments to all of us, as well as let Mother know when all the treatments should get under way. Dr. Jones explained about the radiation treatment that would be needed for the tumors in the head and about the chemotherapy treatments, which would be done in three phases.

Pat asked, "Why three chemotherapy treatments?"

Dr. Jones explained, "Chemotherapy is thought to kill a percentage of the total number of cancer cells. If the chemotherapeutic agents kill a percent of the cancer cells each time, the third treatment your mother undergoes would put the cancer cell count considerably less. So, after a number of treatments the number of cancer cells would be such that the Immune System might, just might, be able to kill the last cells. But of course the lung cancer is not the only cancer in your mother's body. The chemotherapy would have no major impact in the destruction of the twelve tumorous brain cancers. In our body there is what is known as a brain barrier and it is very selective as to what substances gets from the blood to the brain tissue. So as I said the radiation treatment is the best for the brain tumors.

We asked other questions as he went through the methods and the procedures concerning the treatments. When Dr. Jones finished he asked if there were any other questions. There wasn't a word or a sound from any of us. I wanted to get out of there and scream. 'Why? Oh, why is this happening?'

Mother sighed and began to speak, "I'll do the radiation treatments and I'll go through the three phases of chemotherapy but, Dr. Jones, if there is no improvement, I don't want to continue. I also want it understood here and now, there will be no, and I mean no, intervention with machines to prolong my life if that becomes necessary, is that understood?" As she ended, this question she looked from James, to Pat, to Carol and then to me waiting for our response.

The four of us answered in unison, "If that's your wish, Mother. If that's your wish."

Dr. Jones acknowledged, "Mary Alice, it is your decision to make. I am here to help you, whatever you decide you want to do or not to do."

Mother was released from the hospital on Saturday October 7. She would begin the radiation treatment two days later.

On Monday the radiation team at Methodist Hospital led by Dr. Stevenson met with all of us including Carol's husband Dwight, who ask if he could be with us. He always felt that Mother was a second mother to him. They told us how many treatments would be needed and the procedure that would be followed for the thirteen doses of radiation that Mother would be given. This meant that from Monday through Friday Mother would need to be at the hospital's radiation department for her treatment. She would need one of us to be available to take her to these treatments. Dr. Stevenson also told us about the side effects that would probably happen. The main one was loss of appetite. He insisted that her meals consist of a balanced diet. In other words, the meals should be high in protein, high carbohydrate and low in fiber. We should take extra time to make the meals appealing, as Mother's sense of taste would lessen; resting before and after meals would decrease her chances of being nauseated and/or vomiting. He said that she could experience some diarrhea and for that we would need to increase calories and fluids and give a low roughage diet. The other side effect would be alopecia, hair loss. He gave us the name of a shop that specialized in fitting cancer patients with a wig that is as close to the individual's hair as possible. We were also precautioned against having Mother around a lot of people, as her immune system might be low, especially if her white blood count is low. He gave us the telephone number of the American Cancer Society should we need any support items to help with the care of Mother.

The Radiotherapist came in and took us on a tour of the facilities. He described the steps that Mother would go through, from signing in for the treatment, to seeing where she would be when they performed the radiation dosage. The Radiotherapist told Mother that he would be stationed outside the treatment room, where he would perform the treatment, and he would be observing and in communication with her at all times. He explained that the treatment would last from one minute to two minutes. This would be determined by Dr. Stevenson after he reviewed Mother's Medical Records from Dr. Jones. He then asked Mother to come into the room where she would be while the treatment was given. He asked her to cleanse her facial skin thoroughly, then he began to put marks with a marker on Mother's face and neck area. Mother was told that the marks that he put on her head would be his guide throughout the treatments. He advised her not to wash the marks off of her face, during her baths until all treatments were finished. He told Mother that over the period of treatments he would be directing the rays from different angles, to minimize the exposure to normal skin tissue. I listened but my heart was so burdened by what this wonderful woman was going to have to go through.

All I could think about was, 'I'll help you Mother, and I'll do anything and everything that it takes to see you through all of this. I promise you. I promise you.'

Pat went to a few of the treatments, before she left to go back to Texas City. I could see the fear and the hurt that she was enduring as she said good-bye to Mother. "Please let me know if you need me to come back. I know I have my business to look after but you are more important to me than any job or business. Please, Mother, promise me you'll do that," she said.

"I will Pat," was her response.

It was up to Carol and me now to be with Mother on a continual basis at her apartment and to see that she had a way to the Cancer Radiation Department at Methodist Hospital.

By the time Mother had completed five of the thirteen treatments, there was a definite change in her eating habits. She had to be coaxed to eat. I knew it was important to keep her eating well-balanced meals, but there were times when she would say, "Mary Joe, I don't want to eat." And she would push the food away with her hand. When she did, I would pick up the fork and start to feed her. She would dart her eyes at me and say, "I told you I don't want this food."

"O.K. I'll fix you something else," I would reply.

"Don't get smart with me," was her answer.

"I know, Mother, you don't want anything to eat but you must, and I'm going to see that you do." That usually got her to go ahead and finish her meal. The struggle was always there during each meal to get her to eat enough to keep up her strength. My concern was that she still had eight more radiation treatments to go; then would come the chemotherapy treatments and she would have to have her body built up for that procedure. I would think to myself, 'Mother can't you see, I'm not your enemy here.'

I made it a point to call Pat and keep her informed about Mother. On one of those calls, Pat told me about a night she had stayed with Mother. "I woke up and saw Mother walking out of her bedroom, into the living room. She sat down in her rocking chair. I didn't say anything. Mother started crying. I started to say something to her but... I turned on my side, facing in the other direction. I thought, 'This is Mother's time for herself.' It was so hard to lay there and listen to her cry. She never knew I was awake."

On the sixth day Mother and I left her apartment building and as we walked to my car without any warning Mother collapsed in my arms and I lowered her to the ground. Two of her friends saw what happened and rushed out to help me get her into the car. I still had a hospital parking lot permit designated for the cancer area parking, so I parked and went in to get a wheelchair for Mother. She was not able to make the walk to the department for her sixth treatment. After this incident Mother never had the strength to walk on her own for any distance. She was able to use a walker for her trips to the bathroom, which was located a few feet from her bed, but she needed the wheelchair on all other occasions. The American Cancer Society loaned us the support items we needed. Carol made the call to them and the response was prompt in getting the items to Mother that we needed for her care. At first Carol and I could leave Mother alone for a few hours but now that she needed a wheelchair and walker we no longer felt at ease leaving her even for a few minutes. So the time arrived that Mother would have one of her children with her at all times until the day she passed on.

Mother's last radiation treatment was on October twenty-seven. She put a twenty dollar bill into my hand and said, "Mary Joe, go over to the store and pick up two boxes of candy for the doctors and nurses. I want to show them that I appreciate what they've done for me."

"Just like her thinking about what she can do for someone else." I kept repeating to myself as I made the walk to the store.

I also knew that I had an examination at school coming up in two weeks that I had not even started to review for. "Maybe there will be time to study this weekend after Mother's last treatment," I thought as I left the store headed back to Mother's.

I had enrolled in the Nursing Degree Program at Texas Women's University a few months before we found out about Mother's illness. She was very happy that I had started to pursue my nursing education again. I had attended Arkansas Baptist School of Nursing back in 1955–1957, leaving school to get married. It was the policy of the school that you could not be married and stay in training. I knew Mother felt sad that I didn't finish at that time. I always felt she had wanted to be a nurse and, since she couldn't, she wanted me to be the "nurse". I had completed college, getting a Bachelor Degree in Business Administration in 1975. I knew Mother was proud of that but she had always hoped I would continue my nursing program.

I didn't anticipate the demand that would be placed upon me and the rest of the family. To be a care-giver you must be prepared to become more involved as the progression of the illness increases. The time to be in class became a juggle for Carol and me to work out. She had a contract to paint and wallpaper the living quarters of the priests of Saint Thomas in Dallas. She was about half-way through when Mother's illness was first diagnosed. She would cover for me and I would do the same for her in our caring for Mother. I realized that my schooling was suffering; I was missing some classes and when I tried to study at Mother's I found it difficult.

I remember one particular Sunday: Mother was asleep and I was preparing for an examination. James had just left after spending Saturday night with Mother and had just left. I thought, "boy, I will be able to get in a lot of good studying this afternoon. Wrong!

"Mary, could you come and help me to the bathroom." She would call me in to have me take her to the bathroom, or to the living room, to sit and watch T.V. This went on for the next four hours. Studying was out of the question.

The nights were getting worse. She would call me to help her to the bathroom. Just as I would start to drift off to sleep I would hear, "Mary Joe, Mary Joe are you awake. Can you help me to the bathroom, again?" I know it was hard on her as she was not getting her hours of sleep, but neither was I.

"Mary Joe I need----"

'Oh, Mother, I love you so but I need to get some sleep,' I would say, but I would be up, in a flash, to meet her needs. I thought, 'I promised you I would take care of you during this battle. I won't break that promise to you, but this promise that I made, to myself, is not what keeps me going. It is the love I have for you and the wonderful example I have from you, of how a person should live their life, to care about your neighbors and help those less fortunate. This is the way you lived your life, Mother; this is the way I remember you.'

****

One day I was approached by one of the residents at the apartment complex. Geraldine was a woman of color and was in a wheelchair. She began this way, "Mary Joe, you have the most wonderful mother that God put on this earth. Last month I went out into the lobby to see if I could get help from one of the residents. I had lived in the high-rise for about two months and knew most everyone but really didn't know who I could depend on, should I ever need any help. No one was there that I felt I could trust with my problem. I wheeled myself to the door of the crafts room and looked around and my eyes stopped on Mary Dee (as her friends called her). I asked her if I could talk to her for a minute. She got up and came to the door. I began to tell her that it was two weeks before I would receive my Social Security check and I didn't have any food. I asked her if I could borrow some money until the first of the month. She said, 'Geraldine meet me in my apartment in about thirty minutes. I need to clean up here before I leave.'

"When I got to her apartment, she opened the door and invited me in. Two sacks, full of groceries, sat on the table. She walked over and placed five dollars in my hand. 'Now you take the groceries. The money is to get something extra should you need it.'

"I told her, 'I will pay you back the groceries and the money when I get my check, Mary Dee.'

"She replied, 'You don't need to pay me back the groceries, Geraldine, but I would like the five dollars back.'

"As I left her apartment loaded down with the sacks of food she said, 'Geraldine, if you run short of food before pay day, you know where to come.'"

****

This was just one of many stories that I had heard over the years of living in the presence of this extraordinary woman. She was not a woman of financial means. But I do know that no one would ever go hungry if Mother knew that they were in need. Boy could she cook and always kept plenty of food in the pantry. I said many times, not really thinking of the reality, "If Mother ever dies, it must mean that God needs a good cook."

4

The Treatment Takes Its Toll

Mother's body was physically beginning to weaken. I knew that this was not good for the up-coming chemotherapy treatment. Dr. Jones wanted to get under way as soon as possible after the radiation treatments were completed, so he scheduled chemotherapy to begin November 7. We had two weeks before that started. I found out that it was two weeks of an uphill battle with Mother to try to keep her eating the foods that would, physically, build up her body.

The treatment would take a toll on her body. The chemotherapeutic agents that destroy the cancer cells also destroy the good cells, that is the reason that she would probably start to lose her hair. Her leukocyte and thrombocyte count would also be at a drastically low point the seventh to fourteenth day after the chemotherapeutic agents were given. She would be at greater risk at this time for bleeding and infection, such as a respiratory infection. It would take about three weeks to get the count back up, so that Mother would be ready for her second chemotherapy treatment.

Mother had been a smoker since she was twenty-five years old and was still smoking until she completed the radiation treatments when she stopped smoking. She might take a puff now and then but after the chemotherapy she said she just didn't like the taste or smell. I remember that in 1987 I was over at her house and she began talking about wanting to stop smoking. I was surprised with this as I had always known her to be a smoker. She even stated that she might get in touch with my doctor, Dr. Waters, to see if he had some methods to help her stop smoking. To my knowledge she never followed up on this, as she had continued to smoke up to this point.

She entered the hospital on November 7, to start the first phase of the chemotherapy treatments. Mother was upset that she could not walk into the hospital and fussed that she had to be brought in by wheelchair. I could tell that she was very nervous. A lot had happened to Mother since she found out that she had cancer and this trip was one that would be started with needle sticks, obtaining blood samples, and proceed to the chemotherapy infusion being administered intravenously.

The only other time that I can remember Mother getting stuck with a needle was back in 1984, when she had developed an ear infection and I insisted on her seeing my doctor, Dr. Waters. He did a routine office examination and told her that he was going to give her some medication that would clear up the infection. He left the room and Mother turned to me and said, "Mary Joe, where, where did he go." I told her he went to get the solution to give her a shot. When he came back I told Mother that he was going to give the shot in her buttocks. She reluctantly pulled her slacks down and then she held out her arms to me and I took her into my arms and stood there patting her on the back telling her everything was okay, while Dr. Waters gave her the injection.

Immediately upon admission to the hospital Dr. Jones ordered an intravenous solution to be administered to Mother. He wanted to make sure that she was hydrated and that her kidneys were flushing urine output, for seven hours, before starting the chemotherapeutic agents.

We were told that the chemotherapy treatments would be over a three day stay in the hospital. The antineoplastic agents that would be used in Mother's treatments were Etoposide (VP-16) and Cisplatin (Platinol). The first day would be

VP-16, second day VP-16 and Platinol, and day three VP-16. Dr. Jones also ordered Phenergan, Reglan, and Decadron to be given for nausea and to reduce the pressure in her head due to the tumors. Mother had begun to complain of difficulty in breathing, so the doctor ordered respiratory treatments to be started on her. Alupent was the medication of choice as the doctor wanted to dilate the bronchial tubes so as to get the sputum out of Mother's lungs. An arterial-blood-gas test was ordered and the findings showed that oxygen was low in her bloodstream, so oxygen was started right away at 3 liters/min. Mother didn't say anything while all this was going on. How could she; it seemed as though someone was working on her or getting her ready for a test ever since she was admitted. My heart was breaking, seeing her this way. For a person who never had medical problems, this wonderful woman was having her share and then some.

I told Carol that I would remain with Mother the first night of her stay in the hospital. It was around six-thirty in the evening when the nurse came in to start the first chemotherapy agent (VP-16) intravenously. Mother got up and I helped her to the bathroom before the IV catheter was inserted. I noticed that she remained in there longer than usual. "Mother are you alright," I called out.

"Yes, I am Mary Joe, but let them wait until I'm ready and at this moment I'm not ready..."

I knew that she was fearful about the treatments that she would be undertaking the next three days. How could she not be, with all that she had experienced during the radiation treatments?

Then Mother started talking, it was more like yelling to me, "What's going to happen to me after these treatments. I don't want to eat, I'm losing my hair. Oh, Mary Joe, I'm so sick. Is this really worth it?"

I stood outside the door listening and found it hard to put together the words to answer her. 'Oh, Mother it's worth it!! If you weren't going through all this I couldn't talk to you on the phone; wouldn't see your face; couldn't kiss you or hug you.' All this raced through my head before I responded, "Yes, Mother it's worth it." She opened the door and we stood there looking at each other...

Several hours later after the IV had been started Mother complained that her arm that the IV was in was hurting her. No nurse had been in to check on Mothers progress since the chemotherapy treatment had been started. I felt that the nurse should come in and check on Mother. I knew from working with patients receiving chemotherapy that it's very important to closely monitor the IV, to check the IV flow and to check the skin around the catheter for redness, swelling, or drainage. In some cases, if certain chemotherapeutic agents are allowed to leak into the surrounding tissue they could just cause pain or could cause tissue destruction of skin, nerves or muscles. I felt it was about time that a nurse came and checked on my mother. I pushed the nurse call button.

The nurse came into the room and I explained Mother's arm was hurting and that I was concerned that no nurse had been in to check on the IV or how Mother might be tolerating the IV. The nurse appeared genuinely sorry for the way that I felt. We talked for a while, then she left the room.

It was late; Mother and I hadn't talk for quite a while. I looked over toward the bed and realized that she was asleep. I sat back into the chair and my eyes settled on the IV solution dripping and I thought, 'This is going into her veins. The solution will then become like a knight out to slay the cancerous cells... What thoughts I do have these days...'

When the IV was just about finished, I rang the call button so a nurse would come in before the IV ran completely out. She and I talked while she waited for the remainder to run in. She then took out the IV catheter. 'Mother's first day of treatment is over,' I thought. I watched the nurse take down the bag that had contained the chemotherapy agents, she threw it away in the tray can. She didn't wear special gloves for handling chemo products, nor did she secure the IV bag in a marked container, specifically, for those items to be disposed of according to hospital policy. "Oh, god, who will be Mother's nurse for to-morrow's treatment and for those to follow," I spoke under my breath.

The next day I spoke to the supervisor about what had transpired and my concern that there wasn't constant moni-toring of the IV. I informed her, "I work in a hospital and know how busy the nurses can be. My sister and I bathe Mother and we change the linens on her bed. All we ask the staff to do, is to furnish us with the items we need to care for her." The supervi-sor assured me she would handle the problem. I assumed she did, as the remaining two IV chemotherapy treatments given to Mother were continually observed and her vital signs periodi-cally monitored.

After the first chemotherapy treatment Mother urinated only 500 cc of urine, so a Foley catheter was inserted into the bladder. Now she wouldn't have to physically exert herself to go to the bathroom. Also from the time Mother was admitted to the hospital, medication was given routinely to keep her relaxed.

The second day of admission she began to pick, with her fingers, at the sheets and the air. "Mother, what are you doing?"

Her response, "Nothing. Oh, nothing."

The day seemed to pass slowly and as night approached I was ready to sit back in the recliner and relax. I knew Mother would be asleep before long and I would be able to get some sleep. The time came and I drifted off to sleep... but... only for a few minutes. I woke up with the rustling sound of bed sheets. I jumped up from the chair and saw Mother had scooted down to the foot of the bed. All the covers and her gown were off and she lay there 'stripped naked'.

"Mother, for heaven sake, what have you done?" I shouted.

"I'm not doing anything, am I?" She replied with that blank look in her eyes. Then I saw the catheter laying on the bed in a pool of blood.

"Oh, Mother, you have pulled the catheter out!

"I did?" she said meekly.

I pushed the call bell to let the nurse know the catheter had been pulled out. She said she was going to wait until the doctor arrived in the morning to see if he wanted another one inserted. Why was Mother acting like this? I began to keep a closer watch on her movements. Throughout the night and early morning she seemed to be getting better. She was more in tune with her surroundings. Later the nurse came in and inserted a solution medication, through the tubing of a continuous IV that was dripping into Mother's veins. Within thirty minutes Mother was picking at the bed sheets and the air again and she had that blank look in her eyes. I left the room and went to the nurses' desk to let the staff know of her change. Whatever medication was ordered to relax her might be having an adverse reaction. Dr. Jones discontinued the medication. The rest of her stay in the hospital, she was coherent.

5

Call 911

On Friday November 10th, Mother was discharged from the hospital and instead of going back to her home she went to Carol's house. Carol had decided it would be easier on all of us for Mother to be there. And from this time on Mother never went back to her home of ten years.

Now it was up to Carol, James and I to take turns caring for Mother. Living three hundred miles away prevented Pat from helping us but I knew, as did James and Carol that Pat was always here; if not physically present, she was here in her heart.

Mother was back in control, so Mother thought, since she had left the hospital. She was back to refusing to eat her food. She would let us know that she did not appreciate us trying to feed her. There were times that we even demanded that she eat, but Mother would argue that she was not going to eat if she did not want to.

On Saturday, James went over to Carol's to take care of Mother. I went over on Sunday and stayed until Monday evening. I had made up my mind that I would bring my own meals to Carol's. I knew it was hard enough on Carol and her family to have Mother and one of us there all the time, without having the responsibility of feeding us too. I had talked to Carol about this arrangement and requested she have coffee and tea available while I was there. She agreed. She did mention that while James was there she had to feed him.

I went home on Monday evening. I knew that Mother wouldn't be able to come and live with me so there wasn't a need to remodel the garage into an apartment, but I would like to have Mother come over to my house and stay for short visits. It would give Carol a rest from the twenty-four hour activity going on at her house since Mother's arrival. I moved the furniture around in the front bedroom to accommodate Mother's wheelchair and walker. I was ready should Mother want to visit. How could I have known then that there would be no visit? The hospital and Carol's would be the only places Mother would stay ever again.

On Tuesday, Carol let me know Pat had called and was flying to Dallas to help with Mother. She was to arrive that evening but a heavy fog moved into the Houston area and the plane wasn't able to leave until Wednesday morning. Carol picked her up at the airport. I knew Pat wanted to spend time with her, so I told Carol I would be over on Friday, as I had to work at the hospital for the rest of the week.

I arrived about one o'clock. Carol had coffee and tea made. "Mary Joe, Pat and I are going to the mall for the afternoon. I need to get out of the house for a while. Pat wants to buy a few sweatshirts. Mom didn't eat much for breakfast or lunch. Maybe you can get her to eat some oatmeal this afternoon. You know she loves oats."

"I will do my best to get her to eat," I said.

I tried to feed her. She absolutely refused to eat.

Later, in the afternoon, she needed to urinate. The wheelchair was to wide too get into the bathroom. I lifted her out of the wheelchair and carried her to the toilet seat. It was almost impossible for one person to do. Mother's body was dead weight. She couldn't use her legs to support herself at all. I had mentioned to Carol about getting a bedside commode; it would make it easier for us and for Mother to be able to transfer her from the bed to the commode.

Pat and Carol returned around five o'clock and I let them know Mother wouldn't eat no matter how hard I tried to encourage her. "It was a lost cause," I remarked. They left the room. Mother and I talked throughout the evening and many times during the night. At this point, clock time meant nothing. I slept when Mother slept and was awake when she was awake.

Saturday morning I noticed Mother had difficulty in carrying on a conversation. It was as if she was trying to figure out what to say before she would talk, or she would go blank in the middle of our conversation. I never pushed for an explanation about this. I guess I knew that twelve cancerous tumors in her brain would affect her communication skills. There were times when Mother would look straight into my eyes and make the comment, "So sad, so sad. Why, Mary Joe? Why?"

"I don't know, Mother. I just don't know." I assumed she was thinking, "Why was the cancer not detected in December 1988."

I left around noon on Saturday to go home. I had to work the next day. Pat said as I left, "Mary Joe, I will call if there is a change in Mamma's condition."

As I drove home I reflected back to Pat's statement, 'change in Mother's condition'. Cancer! That's her condition. What is going to change that? Will the treatments help? Oh, god, I hope so, but look at the toll the radiation treatments had on her body. I was glad to be home for awhile.

I needed to wash my uniforms and get them ready as I would be working a double shift on Sunday and the evening shift on Tuesday and Wednesday. Between caring for Mother, working and going to school, there was little time to do anything else. It was as though my life was on hold.

That night before I went to bed I called Mother to tell her good night and that I loved her. Pat answered the phone.

"Pat, let me talk to Mother." She put the receiver to Mother's ear. "I wanted to talk to you before I went to sleep. I hope you sleep good tonight. Mother, I love you so much."

"I love you too. Are you coming back over soon?" Mother replied.

"Yes, I will be back over to see you real soon," I said.

A few days later, Pat told me that after Mother hung up the phone from my call she turned to her and said, "Pat, I know you kids love me. Y'all, have always, told me that you loved me. This is not something y'all have just started saying to me because you know I'm sick."

On Monday morning, November 20, after getting out of class I decided to stop at Carol's to see Mother before going on home. I knocked on the front door.

Dwight yelled out, "Door's unlocked, Mary Joe, come on in."

Pat was standing at the kitchen sink, washing dishes and Dwight was in the den watching television.

"Hi, y'all," I said as I walked over to the table where Mother was sitting and gave Mother a kiss on the top of her head. She already had lost a lot of her beautiful gray hair and you could see her scalp. There was a dish of baby food in front of her. "When did Mother start eating baby food, Pat?" I asked as I walked into the kitchen area.

"Well, Mary Joe, she wasn't eating anything we fixed for her and I thought I would try her on some baby food. But she didn't eat it either. I have been trying to get her to eat and, I hate to say this, but I forced her to eat a few bites." Pat stopped washing dishes and turned toward me, "Mary Joe, when I forced Mamma to eat she looked at me with tears in her eyes, and said, 'Pat, my stomach hurts. I can't eat, please don't make me.' I felt so bad that I had forced her to eat those few bites."

I turned toward Mother. "If you don't start eating you are going to have to go back into the hospital."

Mother sat there in her wheelchair, with her head down. She looked like a child being scolded. I walked over and looked down at her. Really looked, her skin color was gray and pallid. I took hold of Mother's hand in mine. The color under her finger nails was blue. She was cold and clammy to touch.

"Mother, how do you feel?"

"Mary Joe, I'm so sick. My stomach hurts really bad. I feel like I need to vomit."

I looked at Pat and Dwight. "Mother doesn't look good at all. I think we should do something."

Dwight spoke, "Do you think we should call the doctor or 9-1-1?"

"Let me call Dr. Thomas and let him know how she looks." I called his office. "Dr. Thomas, I'm calling about my mother, Mary Davidson. This is Mary Joe, I'm over at my sister Carol's house. Mother is cold and clammy and her skin color is gray; she hasn't eaten very much since getting out of the hospital. She is complaining of her stomach hurting her and feels nauseated."

He told me to call 9-1-1 and to get her to the Emergency Room immediately. I hung up the phone and turned to Dwight, "Dr. Thomas said to call 9-1-1."

I dialed the number. For many years I have watched the television show 9-1-1 and now I was making that call. I gave the operator Mother's condition and our location. Within five minutes I heard the sirens and looked outside to see the ambulance and fire truck coming down the street. The Paramedics rushed into the house and lifted Mother out of the wheelchair and onto a stretcher. They began to get her blood pressure, pulse and respiration. They ran an electrocardiogram to check her heart. An oxygen mask was put over her face to give her pure oxygen. As they were wheeling her out to the ambulance, I asked where they were taking her.

"General Hospital," they told me.

"You can't take her to General," I said. I gave the Paramedics a brief version of the problems Mother had at General Hospital in December 1988: "Mother was in that hospital back in 1988 and because of what we view as a wrong diagnosis from the radiology department and her doctor, she is now in this condition."

Pat and Dwight both told them, "No way will we let you take her there."

They put Mother into the ambulance; I got into the front seat to make the trip with Mother. The driver made a call to 9-1-1 that he was taking Mother to Charter Hospital, which was a little farther away.

I looked back into the ambulance where Mother was but I couldn't see her. I shouted out to her over the sounds of the siren, "Mother I'm here in the ambulance with you. We will be at the hospital soon."

At eleven forty-five a.m. the ambulance backed into the Emergency Room driveway. From the time I called 9-1-1 to our arrival at the hospital only twenty minutes had passed. I jumped out of the ambulance and ran toward the back. When I got there the nurses were already taking Mother out of the ambulance. I looked at her face and could tell that she was terrified at what was taking place. I wasn't about to leave her side. I knew that the hospital staff would ask me to wait in the waiting room. When they did, I responded, "I'm not going to leave my mother's side." The nurses didn't object, so I went into the Emergency Room with Mother.

It was as though I had become a part of the stretcher that Mother was lying on, I was pressed so close to it, not wanting to be in the way of the medical team that were working on Mother. There were times when as many as six people were working on her at the same time. I was bent over holding her hand and talking softly to her, trying to assure her that everything was going to be all right, and, more importantly, that I was there with her, that she was not alone. I didn't know if everything was going to be okay. So much had happened in the last two months since the diagnosis of cancer.

The Emergency Room doctor examined Mother immediately and asked me questions concerning Mother's health record. Then she ordered medications to be started. An intravenous solution was started to keep a vein open in case medication needed to be given through the vein. Mother was complaining of hurting above the abdominal area. Demerol was given for the pain. An electrocardiogram was taken to rule out any heart problems. The laboratory technician drew blood to do a complete blood work-up. A respiratory therapist drew blood for an arterial-blood-gas test. Oxygen was increased to three liters per minute once the blood gas results were known. A Foley catheter was inserted into her bladder for direct urine elimination. An x-ray was taken of her chest and the results showed she had pneumonia.

I wondered, 'What else is this woman going to have wrong with her?' The doctor inserted a Levine tube into Mother's stomach and suctioned out 500 cc's of old blood. To me it looked like coffee grounds. I now understood why she was in tears, complaining about her stomach pain. Exhausted from all the tests and procedures, the pain medication helped Mother to relax and she drifted off to sleep.

Pat and Dwight had followed the ambulance to the hospital and were in the waiting room when I walked in to let them know Mother's progress. They wanted to go in and see her, even though I informed them that she was asleep.

Pat went in and when she returned she was crying. "Mary Joe, I didn't realize Mamma was that sick. You know what I mean. All that blood in her stomach. And I forced her to eat... Oh, Mary Joe, I feel so bad about that."

"Pat, you couldn't have known that. Don't blame yourself."

"I'm so glad you came over this morning. What if I let Mother stay at the house that way? I didn't know. I just didn't know, Mary Joe."

As we stood there talking, Carol came rushing into the waiting room. "Mary Joe, Pat, how is Mom?"

"She's resting right now," Pat answered.

Carol went into the Emergency Room, to see for herself and to let Mother know she was there. After several minutes she returned. "You know, as I drove here, all I could think about, was am I going to be too late? Will Mother be dead when I get to the hospital? I didn't think I could get here fast enough." We sat there discussing what had transpired throughout the morning.

At one o'clock Mother's condition had stabilized and the Emergency Room Doctor called Dr. Thomas to inform him that Mother could be transferred to Northwest Medical Hospital, to continue under his care. She was taken by ambulance and once again I rode with her. Pat and Carol followed. When we arrived at the hospital, Mother was taken directly into the Intensive Care Unit. This time I was left standing at closed doors. This was one place the Medical Staff wouldn't let me stay by her side. She was now in their hands. I turned to walk down the hall to the waiting room and there were Pat and Carol coming toward me. "They've taken Mother into the Intensive Care Unit and we will have to wait until the nurses get her admitted, then they will let us in for a few minutes," I said.

At two-thirty we were able to go in to see Mother. James had arrived by that time, so we four walked into her room. There she was, lying on the bed with restraint straps around her wrists tying her to the bed. The nurse told us that Mother had pulled out the Levine Tube that had been put in at Charter Hospital and she was trying to get out of bed, so they felt for Mother's own protection they needed to restrain her. I told the nurse that Mother had an adverse reaction to several medications in her last stay in the hospital. If the doctor had ordered Phenergan or Valium they needed to let him know so he could discontinue them. I found out later that she was getting those medications and the doctor did discontinue them.

Once we left Mother's room I knew we must call her brothers and sisters to let them know what was happening. Pat and Carol left to make the calls.

When they came back Pat said, "Aunt Joan will be here to be with Mother this Wednesday. Aunt Pauline will arrive on Thursday. There wasn't an earlier flight she could get. I guess the airlines are busy with Thanksgiving Holiday this week."

We spent the rest of the day in the waiting room, taking turns visiting Mother at two hour intervals. Pat and Carol left the hospital at about ten o'clock. James and I, feeling completely exhausted, left at one o'clock a.m. to return later in the morning.

Pat and Carol arrived back at the hospital about seven a.m. It would be another hour before they could go in to see Mother. They decided to go down to the cafeteria and have coffee and a roll, as they had left home without eating breakfast.

At eight they returned and hurried into the Intensive Care Unit to Mother's room. The bed where Mother had lain the night before was empty and made-up. Pat grabbed Carol's arm, "My god, Carol, where is Mamma." They both rushed over to the nurses' desk.

"Where is my mother," yelled Carol.

"Who is your mother?" was the response from the nurse.

"Mary Davidson," both said in unison.

"Your mother was transferred to the second floor Medical Unit this morning."

Carol was angry. "That's pretty good. No one told us. We could have been with her." They went up to Mother's room. Pat called me to let me know Mother had been moved from the Intensive Care Unit to the Medical floor. I asked her if she had called James, as I knew he would be going to the hospital that morning. She said she would call him.

Mother had not been responsive since her admission into the hospital. I could tell there were times that she could hear and know we were around her but she wasn't communicating verbally with us and then there were times I knew she didn't know we were there.

Since Thursday was Thanksgiving, I told Pat and Carol I would spend Wednesday night with Mother. Her sister Joan had arrived from Arkansas and also spent the night at the hospital. I could tell that she was very upset when she realized that Mother didn't know who she was or that she was there.

Thanksgiving Day was not the one that Pat had envisioned when she made her decision to spend this holiday with our family in Dallas. It had been seventeen years since Pat had been home during a holiday. When she married Jack, they spent holidays with his children from a previous marriage. Now they were all grown and Pat thought it would be nice for all of us to be together during a holiday weekend. She informed us, back in June, she and her family were going to be with us at Thanksgiving. This was three months before we knew Mother had cancer.

When I got over to Carol's house that afternoon, I could tell that this was not the usual joyous holiday we as a family had experienced over the years. Mother was not here! Mother was terminally ill. While eating turkey and all the trimmings, my thoughts were of Mother lying there in the hospital bed and I started to cry. I had to stop eating as I could not swallow the food; it seem to lodge in my throat. Carol prepared plates of food for Mother and Joan. She knew that Mother wouldn't eat anything but she wanted to take it there just in case.

Aunt Pauline had arrived from Washington State early in the afternoon and was anxious to go to the hospital to see Mother. We all pitched in and cleaned the kitchen. Then Pat, Carol, Pauline and I went to the hospital. Mother was still un-responsive to our presence in the room. The next few days we all took turns staying at the hospital with Mother. Aunt Joan left at the end of the week.

6

Home Under Hospice

The doctor had already told us that Mother would not survive another chemotherapy treatment. We now must remember Mother's wishes. "I'll do the treatments but, if there is no improvement, I don't want to continue, and I don't want intervention with machines to prolong my life." We would now need to work with the doctor and the hospital social worker to engage a hospice agency to help us with Mother when she was ready to leave the hospital.

Mother became incontinent with her bowel movements. I suggested to the nurse, rather than let her lie in stool until she had a chance to attend to Mother, just supply us with the linens and we would clean her up. She made sure that we had plenty of diapers and linens.

When James arrived at the hospital to take care of Mother, I gave him an update on how she was doing. I was concerned as to how he would deal with her incontinence. I told him, "If you hear Mother "pass gas" she has probably had a bowel movement, just call the nurse and she will clean Mother and change her linens."

The next morning when Pat got to the hospital James told her that he had cleaned and changed Mother himself. I knew from experience, working in a hospital, that women care-givers were the ones to perform such tasks. I have never been able to understand why most men won't accept the responsibility of total care for a loved one should an illness such as this occur within their family. I was so proud of James.

Later that evening when the night nurse arrived, Pat asked, "My brother stayed with Mamma last night. How did he do?"

"He did just fine, I believe he slept through most of the night," she replied.

Pat told me later what the nurse said. We both looked at each other, I shook my head, rolled my eyes and let out a sigh, and we looked at each other again and broke into laughter, imagining James sound asleep as she made her nightly rounds. I never told anyone, not even James about the night he stayed with Mother at the hospital.

Mother remained incontinent the rest of the week. With the additional care from her family she did not have a bed sore or breakdown of her skin. One of us was always right there to change her and keep her clean and dry. We also made sure we turned her from side to side and on to her back every two hours to prevent pressure sores.

On November 29, after the holiday, Pat returned to Texas City. James and Carol went back to work. I returned to school and also made arrangements with the hospital to work only on the weekends. It was back to juggling our lives with the normal everyday activities, and to make sure one of us was always there to care for Mother. Aunt Pauline stayed in Dallas to help us in any way she could.

Carol met with the hospital Social Worker for her recommendation of a hospice agency in our area. She called Allcare, a private hospice agency, to inquire about what she would need to do to get Mother into the Allcare Hospice Program. The Administrator explained that a Registered Nurse would be assigned, who, working closely with her doctor, would meet all of Mother's medical needs while living in a home setting. A Social Worker would make home visits at least twice a week, to talk to mother and to counsel any other family members, if needed. A Chaplain was on call at all times for spiritual support. Three times a week a nurse's aide would bathe Mother, help with her personal hygiene and change bed linens. Respiratory and Physical Therapists were available for treatments if they were required. The cost of most medications and treatment would be paid for under the program. Since the hospice program is designed for the terminally ill person to die with dignity at home, the Registered Nurse would not call in a Coroner or have an autopsy performed as the law requires under other circumstances when a person dies at home.

The hospice program is not a final commitment. The family has the option to put the patient back into the hospital if they find they need a rest. Also the program can be discontinued if the family is too overwhelmed by the care involved for their loved one.

Pat returned to Dallas on December 9, but before she left on November 29 we as a family we decided that it would be best to take care of Mother at Carol's home with the help from the hospice personnel. As Mother would be discharged soon, Carol arranged with the Allcare Hospice Agency to have a hospital bed, wheelchair, bedside commode and a respiratory therapy machine for her respiratory treatments of Proventil, to be delivered to her home before Mother's arrival. The day before her discharge Carol asked for a Dobbler pump to assist in Mother's feeding, since she was being fed through a tube from her nose into her stomach.

Mother was responsive and knew that the decision she had made on October 6 not to continue treatment if there were no improvement or if complication arose, was now to be carried out by her children and loved ones. She never appeared to be afraid or fearful of knowing there was nothing else to be done except wait for death to happen.

In the middle of December she did request from Carol, "Please keep me informed daily as to what day it is and what is going on with the family and the world news. I don't want to lose touch with reality."

We made plans to go over to Mother's apartment to pack up her belongings and divide them among family members, according to Mother's wishes. Even though her apartment was small, she had the closet, shelves and corners jam-packed with things she had collected over the years. She was like a pack rat, always saving things, but she would comment often, 'I've got to get rid of some of this stuff and get my apartment in order.' Well, she never got around to doing that and now it was up to us to clear out the apartment and get rid of those very items she talked about. Some of her friends at the high-rise came to the apartment while we were there. It was hard to tell Mother's friends she would not be returning. They shed tears and so did we. It was wonderful to know she was so loved by so many.

Mother was discharged from the hospital on December 11. Pat rode in the ambulance with her to Carol's house. Carol went on ahead to check that everything was ready for Mother's arrival. When she got home the feeding pump wasn't there. She immediately called the Allcare Agency to find out where it was. They told her that the cost of the pump and Mother's Insulin medication were not covered by the program because it was not considered essential for the direct treatment of her cancer. Carol told them everything that has happened to Mother was a result of her illness, be it the cancer or the medications she had to take because of the cancer. Pat told me later that Carol was furious. She telephoned her U.S. Representative and U.S. Senator and told them about Mother's illness and that she had just brought Mother home from the hospital to live out her last days there. Within the hour of Carol's call to her elected officials, Allcare called and said a feeding machine would be delivered and they also let her know all medications would be paid for.

Once we chose to put Mother into the hospice program, we immediately became her primary care-givers. It was up to us to take care of all the needs not met by the hospice people. But for a person to go into the hospice program the primary care-givers don't have to be family. A friend, volunteer or a medical person may be the care-giver. The person may also live in their own home or in a medical institution for the terminally ill.

Carol had converted two bedrooms into one large room a few years prior to all this. This room was a perfect place for Mother to be and for those who would be taking care of her. Carol had put a couch, coffee table and twin bed at the opposite end of the room from Mother's bed and television. The bathroom was located just across the hall from the room. While Mother was awake we kept the television on for her. She had many programs she liked and we made sure those programs were on for her to watch. I believe in the beginning she was aware of them and knew what was going on, but toward the end I don't think so. We also played the tape player with music that Mother liked. One night Pat put the earphones on Mother and played a Kenny G. tape, 'Going Home.' Mother looked at Pat while it was playing and said, "Pretty, louder, pretty. Louder, louder." Pat looked at Mother and begin to cry.

7

Our Last Christmas

Christmas was fourteen days away and Carol had already decorated the outside of her house with Christmas lights. Many times at night when I was caring for Mother I noticed her looking out the window at the lit-up lights. "Pretty, pretty," she would say.

Then, there were times, she just stared out the window and said nothing. 'What is she thinking,' I wondered.

During the next few weeks she made the comment to each of us, "So sad. So sad. Why?"

"I don't know, Mother. I don't know, why," I would respond when I was with her. I didn't know why. I didn't have the answer to why the Government released radiation on thousands of us during World War II when we lived in Richland, Washington. I didn't have the answer to why Dr. Matson didn't put you back into the hospital in the early part of 1989, to find out why you weren't getting any better. I don't know why you have the cancer and why it wasn't detected sooner but I do know this, it is sad, so sad.

Most of Mother's conversations had now become one liners.

"I don't know what you kids are going to do without me," she said to Pat, one evening.

"We are grown adults, Mamma, we will be okay."

"I doubt it," was her reply.

No truer words were ever spoken. I still find myself wanting to seek out her counseling. I miss her so much and my life changed dramatically based on how I now view my life in this world. I now seek to know something about this planet I was born on. I now take time to smell the flowers and to feel the dirt under my feet as I walk my path of life. I don't plan on all those tomorrows but I live each day hoping that when the day is over I truly have lived it the best that I could, bringing happiness to myself and to others.

One evening Mother pulled the feeding tube out from her stomach. The nurse told us she wasn't going to restart it right away. She wanted to see if Mother would eat on her own. We now had to try and get her to eat. It took a lot of coaxing but even at that, she never ate much. However, the feeding tube was never restarted.

It was about this time that Mother began to hallucinate. She would see things in the room. For instance, one day she told Pat, "Who does her hair?"

"What did you say," Pat replied.

"Who does her hair?" repeated Mother.

Pat pointed to the television program that was on, thinking that Mother had seen someone on T.V.

Mother told Pat, "No that person there."

"Here," said Pat. She pointed to a balloon, on top of the television, that had a picture of a wild bushy haired duck on it.

"Yes, who does her hair?"

Pat looked at Mother and couldn't help but break out into laughter.

It was several days before Christmas and I needed to shop for my two sons and three grandchildren. I also wanted to buy a special gift for Mother. She was not going to be with us much longer; what could I choose for her that she would take with her. I remembered that one day, several years ago, when I was over at her apartment, she had asked me to go into her bedroom and get a particular box off the shelf.

I brought it back into the living room. She asked me to open the box. "That pajama suit is what I want to be buried in," she told me.

I looked at her, "You had better write that request down and put with your important papers. You will outlive us all." At that time I really believed that.

'A bed jacket would be a perfect gift,' I thought. I headed to the Mall. After stopping in several lingerie departments, I discovered bed jackets were not a popular item. But I was determined to carry on my quest and headed over to the Galleria. Macy's was not a store I shopped in very often, but, as luck had it, they had several bed jackets. I spotted a beautiful pink quilted jacket. I pulled the pajamas from my box and they were a perfect match. A display of small satin pillows filled with potpourri, were sitting next to the rack, and Natalie, who had gone shopping with me, bought one as a gift for Mother. As we were walking, through the accessories department I saw a white silk turban. I thought, 'Pat might like to give this to Mother. It would cover her scant bit of hair she had left after her radiation and chemotherapy treatments.' I added it to my purchases.

I began to cry right there in the store. I told Natalie, "These Christmas gifts, Mother will be taking with her."

Christmas day, a day of joy and celebration for most, was difficult for our family knowing that this would be our last Christmas with this precious individual.

We always took snapshots, of the five of us when we all got together. Since my friend Natalie is a professional photographer, I had asked her if she would take a family portrait of us during the Thanksgiving Holiday. With Mother's radiation and chemotherapy treatments in progress, this plan had been cancelled. I asked Natalie if she would take some pictures, on Christmas Day, of us together with Mother. It would be difficult, knowing that it would be all that I would have left of Mother: memories on paper. But oh, how wonderful it is to look at them from time to time. A few weeks after Mother's funeral I put together photo albums for Pat, Carol, and James of the pictures that were taken. I still pull out my album to look at those pictures.

At Carol's we opened gifts, took pictures and shared our Christmas meal.

Mother drifted in and out of reality, throughout the day.

When Erin and Shawn, her great-grandchildren, went into Mother's room to sing a couple of Christmas songs to her, a smile came over her face.

We each took turns that day spending time with Mother, savoring the precious moments. It was with a heavy heart that I headed for home that evening.

8

Closer to Them

During the next week there were times when Mother was responsive to us and coherent, and other times her mind appeared to be somewhere else, carrying on conversations with those who we knew had died. One time stands out vividly in my mind.

She was talking to her brother Roy, who had died in 1974. She said, "Roy, Roy, don't leave me this time. Take me with you." She had been heard by others in the family talking to her Mother and her Father. She even talked to my brother in-law's mother, Beulah and his sister, Beverly. They had died several years ago. Mother had known both of them.

I was working at the hospital one night, taking a dinner break. I started to cry. One of the nurse's asked me what was wrong; of course, she knew about Mother.

I said, "I'm so envious of the ones waiting for her. She is closer to them now than she is to us."

Pat's family had come up for the Christmas Holiday and needed to be home by December 30. We knew Pat wanted to spend as much time as she could with Mother before heading back to Texas City. James and I knew that when Pat left it would be up to us to help look after Mother. Time seemed to drag by in some ways, but in others it seem to fly by.

December 30 arrived and time for Pat to go! It was hard for her, as she felt it would be the last time she would see her Mother alive. She went into the room to tell Mother goodbye. She sat down, on the edge of the bed and said, "Mamma, hold me." Mother reached out and put her arms around Pat. Pat did the same. They sat there, holding on tightly to each other. "Mamma, I have to go back to Texas City, but I want to tell you, that you have been a wonderful mamma and I love you so much. I have loved you more than I could ever tell you in words."

Mother replied, "You have been a wonderful daughter, too, Pat, and I love you."

At those words, Pat broke down and sobbed openly. Mother held Pat to her breast. During the past few weeks there were times when Mother was disoriented or confused and didn't recognize those around her. Pat was so happy when Mother called out her name. Mother knew who she was: "Pat".

After Pat left, James and I took turns going over to care for Mother. I would stay at Carol's for a period of twenty- four to thirty-six hour interval's to give Carol and Aunt Pauline a rest. I would still bring my own food. I wanted to make it easier for them. The only thing I did ask her to have was coffee and tea.

I knew it was hard for Carol to take time for herself even when James or I was there, but it was important for her to be able to spend time with her own family, to relax, or be able to leave the house and run errands. As I said earlier, Carol had made the room comfortable for another person to stay and sleep in. I can't express in words how much I appreciated my sister and her family for allowing our mother to live and die with dignity in their home. Carol had installed an intercom system in the room so she could hear her anywhere in the house. We could even monitor Mother breathing.

We continued to take turns with Mother for the next ten days until it was time for Aunt Pauline to go back to Washington. She needed to return home; she had been here since November 23rd. She said her final goodbye's to Mother, knowing that it would be the last time she would see her sister alive. She told us it would be too expensive for her to come back for the funeral.

On Saturday, January 13, Carol called to let me know Mother had stopped eating on Friday morning and she hadn't eaten since and wouldn't even drink water. I asked if I should come over, but she said, "Since you are coming over on Sunday, to take care of mom, I don't think that would be necessary. If I can't get her to eat, I don't think you could."

Later that day the nurse arrived and while she and Carol were in the room Mother began coughing. The nurse gave her a Kleenex. Mother coughed up blood. She looked down and saw the blood.

I called from work to see how things were. Carol let me know about Mother coughing up blood.

Then she said, "There was such a sad look in Mom's eyes when she saw the blood. After the nurse left Mom turned to me and said, 'Why? Why did this have to happen to me?' I shook my head then I asked Mom if she wanted me to read the Lord's Prayer. She nodded her head yes. I read it to Mom word for word. Sometimes I just don't know how to answer Mom."

"I know what you mean," I response.

On Sunday morning I called Carol, "I'll be over at four o'clock."

"Mom's friend Liz and her mother Marie are coming over at six. Why don't you wait and come over after their visit," replied Carol.

"O.K., that sounds good. It'll give them some time alone with Mother."

At seven-thirty that evening I called back. "Carol are they still there?"

"Yes, Mary Joe, but come on over anyway, I'm going to the airport, later to pick up Pat, she's arriving at ten o'clock."

I was puzzled, 'Pat's coming back, why? What was going on?' I thought to myself as I got ready to leave my house. I had been at work for the last four days and hadn't seen Mother.

When I arrived at Carol's at eight she told me, "Mom still hasn't eaten nor drunk any water. She is getting worse. I called Pat this afternoon, after I talked to you, to let her know about Mom. She called me back within a half hour to let me know she already had purchased a plane ticket and would be arriving in Dallas at ten o'clock. I've called James and told him about Mom's deteriorating condition. I knew you were coming over, so I decided to fill you in on all that was happening when you got here."

We talked for a while then Liz and Carol left for the airport to get Pat.

I tried to get Mother to drink some water but she would just turn her head away when I put the glass up to her lips. I told her, "Mother, you must start eating and drinking some liquids." There was no response from her.

At eleven o'clock Pat arrived. We all talked about the fact that Mother must start eating, but we knew in our hearts that Mother's time with us was coming to an end. She had lost so much weight; I'm sure, at that time, she couldn't have weighed more than 90 lbs.

We talked for a while longer, then Liz and Marie said their goodbyes and said they would be back Wednesday evening. Liz was like family to us and wanted to keep in close touch with Mother.

9

The Vigil Begins

At one-thirty a.m. on Monday January 15, 1990 James arrived. All of Mother's children were with her now. We began a vigil without realizing it. James and I sat, at the side of Mother's bed, across from each other. Pat and Carol sat on the couch and talked for a while. Then they bedded down for the night, on the couch and the bed located at the opposite end of the room.

James and I talked throughout the night and when Mother would wake up we always let her know, "We're all here with you Mother. Your kids are with you. Mother, we love you, but you know that."

She was so weak, but she would manage or try to say, "I love y'all too."

Monday morning Carol and Pat woke up around eight o'clock and went into the kitchen to fix breakfast. Pat brought James and me a plate of food, while Carol made a telephone call to the Registered Nurse to give her an update on Mother's condition. The nurse told Carol she would be over to the house later that morning.

Pat and Carol took this time to take their bath and straighten up Mother's room. I gave Mother a sponge bath and changed her bed linens. I asked her if she would eat some oatmeal if I cooked her some. She nodded her head, yes. I no sooner got the words out of my mouth than the nurse arrived.

The nurse listened to Mother's heart, through the stethoscope, and informed us the beat was quite rapid, one hundred and fifty times a minute. She told us it would only be a matter of time before Mother died. She said not to force Mother to eat or drink. She then pulled out from her nurse's bag a bottle of Roxanall, Morphine. She told us it was to be given under Mother's tongue with a medicine dropper. "Give 1/2 cc at a time. Don't worry about giving her any of her other medications. Increase the dose if the 1/2 cc doesn't keep her relaxed and comfortable. The purpose is to let her go with as little pain as possible."

"What if I give her too much," Pat asked. I could tell Pat was still uncomfortable about giving Mother her medicine.

"Then she will just go to sleep and not wake up. She will just die," was the nurse's answer. "Do you all want me to stay for a while?"

Carol answered, "No, I believe we'll be okay for now. We might need you later on. I know you told me you would be available day or night should I need your help."

Later Monday morning James, called his work and I heard him tell them, "My mother is dying. I'll be with her until she is gone. If you need to talk to me, this is the phone number, where you can reach me." I had already laid down on the bed to try and get some sleep, when he came back into the room. I told him that night would come sooner than we realized and we needed to be ready to care for Mother through the night. He laid down on the couch and soon we were both asleep.

Pat woke us up at seven o'clock that evening. I got up and went into the bathroom to take a shower and freshen up before James and I took over Mother's care. Pat brought some food into the bedroom. We ate, but each bite was hard for me to swallow. My thoughts went back to the morning. 'Oh, Mother, you wanted some oatmeal but the nurse arrived and I forgot about it. But, would you have eaten it? Mother, Mother I'm so sorry I forgot.' I began to sob aloud. James looked over at me but didn't say anything. I guess he was in his own world of thoughts.

I called the hospital where I worked and told them, "I will be with my mother until she dies. She has not eaten or drunk anything for four days. I don't think it will be much longer before she is gone, but until that happens I want to be with her for as long as I can."

I hung up the phone, turned and looked at Mother and then at Carol, Pat, and James. There we were, the five of us, one waiting for death to take over and four watching, loving, touching, talking to this woman whom we had loved and known for the existence of each of our individual lives as Mother.

Carol's family took on the sole responsibility of feeding us. They were wonderful and I know it was a strain on them, too. They, too, loved Mother dearly.

We were each in our own world of memories and what we might say to Mother when she was awake. Now that we were giving her the Morphine under her tongue there were three to four hours she would be asleep. The only thing we requested from each other was, "If I'm asleep when Mother wakes up, wake me up. I want to be able to talk to her and see her when she is awake." Sometimes it seemed she recognized us and then sometimes I knew she didn't.

During Monday night and early Tuesday morning hours James and I sat up to care for Mother. Each time she woke up we would wake up Pat and Carol. We would all stand around the bed talking, crying, touching and holding on to her. Then, when it looked as if Mother was getting anxious or agitated, we would look at each other, each crying, and would say, "We need to give her the Morphine." It was so hard to do because she would go back to sleep for three to four more hours. We were very selfish of her time now, but it was all we had left. I wanted to keep her awake for as long as I could, just to be able to look into her eyes and have her see me. When the Morphine took affect her eyes would close.

My, niece, Ginger had given Mother a little cross the last time she was in the hospital. James had placed it on Mother's chest. It wasn't on a chain so each of us had to continually place it on her chest when it slipped off. Carol had brought her a little white Bible during this time. Mother took it and held on to it constantly, except for the time Carol would take it and read scriptures to her.

Mother never talked to me about her religious beliefs. I knew she was a member of the Methodist Church. She wasn't a church goer, but the way she lived her life was one filled with care and compassion for others. As little as Mother had, there was always something for those who had less than herself.

Eight o'clock Tuesday morning Pat and Carol were up and getting ready to start the day caring for Mother while James and I thought of getting some sleep. We both knew that sleep for us was only while this loving person had her eyes closed. When her eyes opened up, Pat or Carol would wake us so we could be right there by her bedside, getting one more treasured moment with Mother.

During the day the nurse came by to see Mother. After listening to Mother's heart and getting an update from Pat and Carol on Mother's status, the nurse commented, "It won't be long, but I've said that before and look at how long she has lasted. It is impossible to give a certain time for death. When it is time, it happens." She stayed for a while talking with Pat and Carol, letting them know before she left that she was available day or night.

Every once in a while Pat or Carol would leave the room to take a smoke break. They felt it best not to smoke in Mother's room and, also, James and I were non-smokers.

James and I lay down and were soon asleep, but throughout the rest of the day we were awakened twice by Pat or Carol. Sleep was needed but there would be time for that later. Time was running out for these precious moments to be able to talk and be with Mother.

Before she went to sleep that night, Pat told me that she noticed Mother on several occasions put her finger between the pages of the little white Bible. And even though Mother appeared to be asleep, Pat said she could hear Mother say, "Uh, Huh." She told me, "It was like Mamma was hearing someone, and it had to do with what was in the Bible pages. She did this several times throughout the day."

Wednesday morning Mother's brothers and sister called, from Arkansas to see what was going on with Mother. We told them they might want to stay close to their home, as we would probably be calling them soon to let them know that Mother had passed on. They expected as much but they were still in disbelief that their sister was this ill. Their mother, Annie, had lived to be ninety-one. I guess they thought Mother would do the same. I know I had thought she might outlive some of us, her own children.

Later in the evening Liz and Marie came over to see Mother and just be with us. Before they left we had prayer led by Liz. I remember it as if it was yesterday she said, "Lord, comfort Mary's family. Show them, Lord, your mighty powers."

10

Tell Us Goodbye

Thursday morning about three o'clock, Mother woke up. James went over and woke up Pat and Carol. "Mom is awake and it looks like she might know what is going on."

Both jumped up and ran over to Mother's bed. They started to talk to her, "Mamma, we love you."

In a low muffled sound "I wove wo too," was her response.

When she said those words, even though the pronunciation was incorrect, we all knew what she said. She started turning her head, to be able to look at each one of us. I could tell that it was a strain on her to do this. About that time, James said, "Let's stand at the foot of the bed, so Mom doesn't have to turn her head." There we stood, all of us looking at our Mother. She was looking at us... at me... We were talking and crying at the same time.

"Mother, tell us goodbye," we said in unison. She didn't respond.

Then James spoke, "Mom, if you're not going to tell us goodbye, give us that sweet little smile we all know."

My mother smiled. We broke down, crying openly. What a smile, I will never forget it. My heart was joyful and breaking at the same time.

We talked to Mother for a while longer, then her left arm began to jerk quite rapidly. We looked at each other, knowing it was time to give Mother the Morphine. We were crying uncontrollably, knowing we had to give it but wanting this moment of being close again with Mother to last... Pat, tears streaming down her face, gave the Morphine to Mother under her tongue, while Carol ran into the bathroom and brought four washcloths and gave each of us one. There we four stood, at the foot of the bed, crying and telling Mother we loved her. Mother lay there in her bed looking at us... then... her eyes closed.

That was the last time Mother was responsive to us. Even though Mother's eyes were closed, we always talked to her hoping and thinking she might hear us and know that we were there.

Pat and Carol did not go back to bed. Mother's condition began to change drastically over the next few hours. Her breathing became shallow and uneven, more like gulping for air. I picked up the stethoscope and listened to Mother's heart rate. The count was down to about forty beats a minute. I told the others.

They leaned over the bed, hovering over Mother, realizing that the end was near. I kept the stethoscope earpiece in my ears. Mother's heart stopped beating. I yelled at the others, "Her heart has stopped!"

I jerked the stethoscope off. I grabbed for any part of Mother that I could latch on to, screaming, "Mamma, Mamma, Mammaaa." I couldn't see anything as my eyes were so full of tears.

Even, over my screams, I could hear James, Pat and Carol crying and screaming, Mother's name and could feel Mother's body being tugged by them. We had said we were ready to let her go, but when Mother's heart stopped beating we all grabbed onto parts of her body. There we were, crying and holding on to her.

Several minutes went by and no end in sight to the crying and grabbing, by each of us, for Mother's body. All of a sudden, I heard a heavy sigh, coming from Mother? I looked down. Mother was back breathing again. I could not believe it! She was back! And we said we were ready to let her go. I think not.

Later that morning we talked about what had happened just a few hours earlier, and we knew that we were going to have to let Mother go. We couldn't say, 'Yes we're ready to let her go' and then hold on to her as she passed on. Carol took hold of Mother's left hand, and I took hold of Mother's right hand. Then we joined hands with James and Pat. We had created a family circle. A circle that would be broken by the death of our mother. Each one of us stood there and one by one made the commitment to let Mother go.

I laid down on the bed and was soon asleep. I was able to sleep for a few hours. When I woke up I got out of bed and walked over and sat down in the chair to the left of Mother. I just wanted to be near Mother.

11

Letting Go

I was standing near the window watching the rain come down. It had been raining for the past two days. I looked over at Mother, then back outside. "They are crying in Heaven for Mother," I said out loud. I looked at Pat. She glanced up with a puzzled look on her face. "The rain is really tears," I said as I turned, once again, to look outside. I didn't say anything else and Pat didn't comment on what I had said. But what else needed to be said?

It was about three o'clock in the afternoon. The rain had stopped. I was sitting on the couch and Pat was sitting next to Mother. Carol's dog Saber came into the room and went over to the left side of the bed. She laid her head on the edge and looked at Mother. Pat said, "What's the matter Saber?" I looked over at Saber, she was shivering. Pat called her over and gave her some pats. The dog looked over at Mother and walked out of the room. "I wonder what was wrong with Saber," Pat repeated.

Natalie arrived about four-thirty in the afternoon. She tried to get over or call at least every other day to see if we needed anything or to run any errands for us. I talked to her about what had happened to Mother that morning.

Natalie told me about something strange that had happened Monday evening:

"Sabrina, a woman that I had met through a spiritual workshop, called me. We both had moved and had lost contact with each other during the past year. Sabrina, now living in California, had gotten my phone number from a mutual friend in New York. For some reason, during our conversation, I told her, 'Mary Joe's mother is dying, and she has been with her, at her sister's, since Sunday.'

"Sabrina told me she has been with several people when the spirit has passed on. Sabrina explained that it's quite a remarkable experience to be there but it's important to let the spirit go, as it no longer needs the physical body. If the spirit is not able to leave, when the time comes, it becomes painful for that physical body.

"Then, I told her, I would pass that on to Mary Joe and said it was good hearing from her."

I then told Natalie how James, Pat, Carol and I joined hands with each other and with Mother and made the commitment to let Mother go when she passes on, again.

"Natalie, she was gone, free from all pain forever. We might have been responsible for bringing her back, through our grabbing and holding on to her physical body, not letting her spirit pass on."

We talked for a while longer, then I left the living room and went back into Mother's room.

12

One Last Gift

"**N**OTE TO THE READER." *These moments are impossible to speak of as if they are in the past; they still feel really "present" as if it happened yesterday.*

For the sake of clarity I have used italics to set apart what I witnessed and others witnessed from my narration of the ordinary events. Where Pat or Carol are telling what they saw from their own point of view, I have begun the paragraph with the speakers name in parenthesis. In these italicized sections, the pronoun I refers to the person who is recounting her experience. These parts are written in present tense. As I write what happened over the next five and one half hours in Mother's room I feel as if I'm there again.

(Mary Joe)

Pat and James are sitting on either side of Mother's bed. Carol is sitting on an ottoman, and I'm standing at the foot of the bed to the left of Carol. The room is dark except for a small light on a dresser behind James. It is around five o'clock and already getting dark outside. Mother is gulping for every bit of air she can get into her lungs. It is so hard watching and I'm so full of emotions witnessing her battle to hang on to life.

My eyes are filled with the full image of my mother lying there on the bed. Her body is stiff and rigid; her head is arched back and pressed deep into the pillow. It is so quiet.

I begin to see movement above Mother's body. 'What in the world is going on?' I think. Then all of a sudden Mother's bed is all lit up with rays of gold and crystal clear light radiating on, above and around the bed. My mouth opens in amazement at what is happening. I can't believe what I'm seeing. . . but I don't know what I'm seeing. I see all this going on and I see Mother's body lying there. Then this electrical like activity becomes so intense that I can't see Mother's body anymore.

I leave the room and rush down the hallway to the living room, where Natalie is sitting on the couch. "Natalie, something is happening in Mother's room. I am seeing rays of light everywhere and one time I couldn't see Mother because of light streaking all above her body. What do you think it is?"

"I don't know. But whatever it is, go back in there and be open to what you are seeing."

(Mary Joe)

I hurry back into the room. I stand at the foot of the bed hoping and wondering, if what I saw, just moments before, was going to happen again. I don't have to wait long for the answer.

The wall behind Mother, is no longer a wall that I'm looking at. There are no corners or ceiling in view. It is as though, I'm standing back and looking into an area that has infinite depth. Behind, above and on both sides of Mother glow the whitest white light I have ever seen. I look at Mother. Illuminating around the top of her head is an aura-like halo. Then as I look straight ahead into the white light, bands of Gold appear in the distance. From where I'm standing, forward, the area is all lit up with this brilliant array of white light and gold. The white light is bright but relaxing to my eyes. I'm in awe as to what is happening. I know that what I'm seeing is not of this World, but I'm not afraid.

My eyes settle back on Mother. In a flash, there are beams of crystal clear light shooting outward in all direction from a centered area located above Mother. In between the beams there are numerous round objects, like the tops of people's heads. With all this energy going on I can't see Mother on the bed. My heart is out of control; it is pounding faster and louder. There is Mother's body again. I can see her. Oh, what is going on? It is as though I'm in a trance. There is movement going on just above Mother. I look really hard to see what it is but I don't have to. It shows me. My mother's spirit moves to the left of her and floats over to the edge of the bed. It then shoots back above Mother's body.

I gasped, turned and run out of the room, down the hallway to where Natalie was. "Natalie, I'm seeing white light everywhere and Natalie, I just saw Mother's spirit. I could see Mother's body and could see her to the left of herself. What I'm seeing no one is supposed to see."

"Who said?" was her reply.

"I don't know." And with that response I run down the hallway and back into the room.

(Mary Joe)
Am I going to have the privilege to see anymore of the glorious and magnificent scenes I have already been blessed to witness? The answer is yes. Moments after getting back into the room, the spectacular events begin to unfold again. Movement over Mother; I get to see more! The force responsible for what is going on in that room, is like a magnet drawing me more and more

into the splendor of each glorious moment that my eyes behold. Mother's spirit is on the move. It glides over the bed with such ease, going to the right of Mother and to left, always stopping at the edge. Several more times Mother's body is blocked from my view by the voltaic energy exploding, shooting beams of crystal clear light and gold streaks across and above her bed. Activity is accelerating as I move mentally into this majestic drama being played out in front of me. The star is Mary Alice Davidson. The director is her Lord. I am the spectator for this one time showing. I have a front row seat.

At this point I hadn't said anything to the others in the room. 'Should I say anything to them about what I'm seeing? What if I don't and Mother dies and then I tell them? Will they be mad or upset?' All this was racing through my mind as I watched the 'spirit' move freely over the bed.

(Pat)
I told Mary Joe, I knew, something was happening. "I noticed you leaving the room several times and returning. I was watching you and your mouth and your eyes would open wide like you were surprised or that you saw something. I thought, 'What is she doing?'"

Finally I have to speak up. "I don't know whether I should say this or not because y'all are going to think I'm crazy but I have to tell y'all what I'm seeing. I'm seeing Mother's spirit. It's is about six inches above Mother. I have watched it go from the left and the right side of Mother to the edge of the bed. Sometimes in a flash it returns hovering directly over Mother."

"That's nice, Mary Joe, but all I see is my mother's body," James said.

James, Pat and Carol left the room.

I know when they left but it is as if they were apart from me and where I am. I was drawn to the action taking place in front of me. I didn't want to lose sight of my Mother's spirit or lose the restful feeling that was within me. It was like standing on the edge of the world looking into another dimension.

(Pat)

The three of us leave mother's room and go into the kitchen. James began to tell Jack, "Mary Joe's in there saying she sees Mother's spirit."

"Well, James you never can tell, maybe she does." I'm not saying that she doesn't see something, Pat. "I guess people can see what they want to see. But all I see is Mother lying there."

"Well, I haven't seen anything and I want to get back in there." I say as I headed down the hall.

(Mary Joe)

I never was aware of when they came back. I know I was watching the 'spirit' drifting over to the left, to the edge of the bed. Up until now all activity had been confined on, above or around the bed.

I said, "Pat, she's coming toward you."

This time the 'spirit' doesn't stop at the edge. In a split second, the 'spirit' soars off the bed. I'm startled by what I see. It leaves the bed in the form of a perfect square. The background, inside the square, is the whitest white I have ever seen. And within this square is a face. The eyes are dark. The hair is long and wavy. The 'spirit' is looking straight at me with piercing but tender eyes. The mouth is shaped like a triangle. The 'spirit' darts behind Pat, who is sitting in a chair beside the bed.

"Pat, the 'spirit' is behind you," I shout.

(Pat)

I jerk my head around toward the back, but all I see is the wall. I think to myself, 'What in the world is Mary Joe talking about?'

(Mary Joe)

Unbelievable things are happening before my eyes. The 'spirit' went behind Pat but, now it's there in front of her chest. The face, inside the square, is looking at me. The mouth is moving as though it is talking to me it looks happy. A feeling of contentment flows through my body. 'This beautiful face is having fun... with me,' I think.

"Pat, the spirit is in your chest." She looks down at her chest, and sees nothing!

I'm looking at Pat. There is a brightness about her. I stare, in wonderment at what I see. Pat's body is completely enclosed with the white light. I can see the light at Pat's feet. But... how can I, the bed is in the way. My eyes can see everything on this stage that is lit up. Even when I look directly at Mother, I can see James and Pat sitting to the right and to the left of Mother as if I'm in front of each one looking straight at them. What wondrous scenes my eyes have been able to gaze upon.

'All this is impossible, this is heaven at work,' are the thoughts racing through my mind and yet my mind is free, from all but what I'm experiencing.

This pageant isn't for my eyes only. The other spectators have arrived and taken their seats, to behold this grand drama.

(Pat)

I look at Mother. There is a haze directly over Mother's body. I look around to see if anyone has been smoking in the room. No, it isn't cigarette smoke. I look toward an open window to see if dust is coming in. No, it isn't dust. Then I look back at Mother, and from Mother's nostrils and her mouth, rolling clouds of mist were pouring out. I watch mist travel down toward Mother's feet and settle above the length her body.

"Carol, get over in my chair and look above Mamma," I scream as I jump from the chair and head for the hallway, grabbing Mary Joe by the collar as I run by.

"What you're seeing, is it like a haze over Mamma? Like cigarette smoke?"

"No, Pat. I see Mother's spirit lying above but next to her."

"I don't see that," was my response.

As we returned to the room Carol was jumping out of the chair, yelling, "James get over here and look above Mom."

(Carol)

I see a haze just above and the length of Mother's body. James hurries over and looks above Mother's body. "I don't see anything," he responds, returning to the chair where he had been sitting.

I am ecstatic. Pat and Carol has seen something!

I sat down in the chair to the left of Mother to see if I could see what Pat and Carol did. I didn't. Pat stood at the foot of the bed. Carol sat on the ottoman to the right of Pat.

(Pat)

I look at Mother. Nothing. I look again. Nothing! I think to myself, 'Well, whatever Mary Joe is seeing I'm not seeing.' I look toward Mother for a third time.

At about this time the room lights up with whitest white light and gold rays of light in front of me, and there is movement above Mamma. I'm hypnotized to what is going on. I move more to the foot of Mamma's bed and notice that the room is getting larger, wider and the white light brighter. Mamma is lying on the bed. Beams of white light are shooting all over the top of the bed.

Pat began crying, tears running down her face. Her arms lifted upward and hands clutched tightly, "Oh, sweet Jesus, sweet Jesus," she cried. I knew she was seeing something majestic. The moment was broken, for me, by James leaving the room. Evidently it didn't for Pat; it seemed she was in a world of her own.

Carol moved over into James's chair. I was sitting to the left of Mother. Pat was not saying anything to us but I could tell from her facial expressions that she was still seeing something.

(Pat)

I'm watching the activity happening in front of me but I can see Carol all lit up with an aura from the top of her head to her feet forming a complete outline of her body. Carol is wearing a red outfit and Mary Joe has on black. Mary Joe is engulfed in a bright light from head to toe. I look more at Mamma, grayish light and streaks of silver are shooting in all directions, above and around the edge of the bed. Mamma has a bright white light around her head.

I had to get back to the foot of the bed, where the best seats in the theater were, so to speak. James has come back into the room. He and Carol are standing together at the left side of Mother. Pat remains at the foot of the bed along side me.

(Mary Joe)
"Carol, Mother's 'spirit' is moving toward you," I said. Carol has her right hand resting on Mother's arm. "Carol the 'spirit' is traveling up your arm. Oh, Carol you are cradling the 'spirit' in your arm." What an incredible sight; Carol holding onto Mother's arm and cradling the 'spirit' at the same time. 'Carol looks down and sees a bright white glow at her elbow.'

(Mary Joe)
"James the 'spirit' is coming toward you. It's off the bed going up your arm." The 'spirit' shoots off the bed, in a flash, and is once more in the form of a perfect square. Inside the square is a brilliant white background. The face. The face is there!! Oh, God, I get to see that precious face once more. Those beautiful dark piercing eyes are looking at me. Oh, how wonderful it makes me feel. I feel so close and connected to this divine spiritual being. My eyes are focused on nothing else but the face, dark nose, the dark triangular shaped mouth and the long, wavy, dark hair.

The 'spirit' travels up James' arm and then, almost as if it knew it has come to his heart, it stops.

"James the 'spirit' is in your heart," I whisper as tears fall from my chin. 'Its' little mouth just moving as if talking to me and deep within me, I knew it was saying, 'Oh, Mary Joe this is so peaceful. I feel so alive and free.'

I believe I could live the rest of my life in this splendor. I want it to keep going on and on and on.

(Carol)

I'm sitting at the foot of the bed on an ottoman to the right of Mary Joe. All is quiet in the room. My eyes are on my wonderful and loving mom. I glance outside; it is dark and it is sprinkling rain. It won't be long before Aunt Pauline's plane arrives at the airport. She had just left less than two weeks ago and said she wouldn't be able to come back for the funeral. But when I called on Monday to let her know Mom's condition she told me she was coming back. Richard is probably already at the airport to pick her up. I turn back to Mom. 'Hang on Mom. Just hang on, Aunt Pauline will be here soon.' These thoughts are rushing through my mind, when I realize there is bright white light all around Mom's head. It is as if she had a halo above her head. 'What is that behind Mom's head?' I lean forward and strain to make out what it is. It looks like little children jumping up behind and around Mom. They are looking at her. It is as though they are straining to see Mom's face!

This will be the last time I personally will see these glorious events. But the magnificent panoramic views I was so privileged to see, are now embedded in my brain. I have the pleasure of seeing these scenes over and over again from now on for the rest of my life.

James remains with us in the room until just before Aunt Pauline arrives from the airport, but he never he indicates that he sees anything other than Mother's body.

I hadn't left the room since ten after five. I don't want to miss the powerful and moving events taking place in this room.

(Carol)

I look over at James, his hands are covering his face, elbows on the bed, and he is crying openly. Then I see a movement and realize that what I am seeing looks like a glowing face flowing toward James in a soft wavy motion with a white charcoal bright light trailing behind it. "James, it's coming toward you. It's going between your arms." Then it shoots into his chest.

"I hope it is with me," he sobs.

(Pat)

I'm standing there looking at Mamma's spirit right above her body. The 'spirit' shoots upward from Mamma's head and comes, real fast, right to me and stops at the foot of the bed. It is a complete square. It is just as white as it could be. There is a face inside the square. The hair is really wavy. The eyes, nose, and the mouth are black. The little face is within two feet of me. I could reach out and touch it. 'Its' mouth is opening and closing as if it is talking to me. I can't believe what I 'm seeing. A square with a face inside it. But I feel the fullness of a complete being before me. And my head and heart swim with the wonderment of it all. Its eyes look into my eyes and, I feel, into my heart as well. It looks so at peace with itself.

I want to talk directly to it, and say, "Hi, how are you?" But I don't. As fast as it traveled to the foot of the bed, it returns like a flash back into Mamma.

Mother is getting worse. Her breathing is very shallow and weak. Mother is going.

James was getting all excited, "Hold on Mom. Aunt Pauline is coming". As he leaves the room he says, "I'm going outside to wait for Aunt Pauline." We know that she is en route from the airport.

(Pat)

It is about ten thirty p.m. Mary Joe is sitting to the left of Mamma, Carol on the right and I'm at the foot of the bed. In front of me is misty looking but all around is sparkling with the brightness of the White Light that has appeared. Mary Joe and Carol each are encircled from head to toe with the bright light. My eyes catch movement behind Mary Joe. I look.

"Ohhh, they are coming for Mamma. I think it's almost time," I said.

"Why?" Mary Joe replied.

"There are two figures dressed in white behind you. Way taller than you. They're behind you, Mary Joe, and back there is as golden as golden can be."

"I want to see," I cried as I jump from my chair and rush to stand next to Pat. I focus on the area behind the chair I had just been sitting in. I gaze into a radiant glow of white light and a brilliant band of gold. I want so badly to see what Pat is talking about but I never see the two figures. I stand there for a few more minutes but I can tell Mother is nearing the end and I want to be there next to her when she dies. I sit back down beside Mother.

(Pat)
Mary Joe gets up from her chair it is like a spotlight is shining directly down on the chair where she was sitting a moment ago. Even though the color of the chair is black, everything in that area is a bright white light. When she went back and sat down she immediately was framed in bright light from head to foot."

My eyes are on the two figures. 'Who are they?' is the thought racing through my mind, as I begin to see a third figure appearing behind Mary Joe. It is taller than the other two. I'm beside myself with emotion. I scream, "I'm telling you, they're coming. They're here to get Mamma!! There is a third figure behind you Mary Joe."

(Mary Joe)
I look at Pat and shout, "They can't have her." I throw back my right arm, behind the chair. What is wrong with my arm? I jerk my arm back and look at it. It feels like my arm has entered an electrical field; leaving a tingling sensation, with the hair on my arm standing on end.

(Pat)
My concentration shifts to the right of Mamma. I watch Carol holding onto Mamma's right arm. She begins to bring her hand

up and down on Mamma arm. I see her hand go from Mamma up through the 'spirit' and back through the 'spirit' and return to Mamma's arm.

(Carol)

I grab for Mom's arm yelling, "Just wait Mom; Aunt Pauline is coming. Just, hang in there." I begin to bring my hands up from Mom's arm and return them in a rapid motion. I look down as I return my hands to Mom's arm. There is a fog-like, gray mist just above Mom. My hands disappear into it then I feel my hands on Mom. I release my hold and my hands reappear through the mist. There are my hands! Each time I reach down to grab a hold of Mom my hands disappear into the gray mist. There is Mom's arm; I grab it, then I bring my hands up and out of the mist again.

A car pulled up outside.

(Pat)

My eyes are fixed on what is going on in the foreground. Instead of bright light a gray haze fills the area before my eyes. There is movement over Mamma. No sooner do I see the movement, I see the 'spirit' rising up. This time, it is not a face in a square, this is my mamma. Its body is young but there is no doubt, I know it is my mamma. She is wearing a long flowing white garment. What's that on her sides? I look closely and think, 'Wings?' No, it must be the pillow. But it can't be the pillow because I see Mamma's body and the pillow through her 'spirit.' And then I see wings.

"She has wings! She has wings! She is beautiful, just beautiful." Tears are streaming down my face.

(Mary Joe)

"Wings? Pat said wings!" I slid out of the chair to the floor, on my knees, my arms outstretched, and crying loudly, "Mother has wings."

Pat nods her head yes.

"My mother has wings!" I cry. No holding back the emotions Mother is on her way home. From my eyes flowed tears of sadness, joy, grief, anger, happiness, love, and praise. My mother is going home in glory!

(Pat)

I follow the 'spirit' with loving and tear-filled eyes as it glides toward me. The very essence of me takes in this beautiful spirit, my mamma. She is young. Her hair is dark, long and wavy. Her garment is misty white, long and flows freely as she heads my way. Extending upward and outward past her sides are wings of the utmost brilliance. The sparkling silver wings continue just past her waist. Her eyes, I see my mamma's beautiful eyes but she doesn't acknowledge my presence.

She is so close to me I could reach out and take her in my arms but it's not my arms that will hold her tonight. She will be in the arms of her Lord. This is no longer her home. Her home is just a step away. She turns toward the three white figures draped in white, waiting for her. Oh, God, what a breathtaking sight. The glowing wings are open and full at her back. Her hair is swept back, downward and resting on the nape of her neck. She is pure perfection. This was my momma. No, this is my momma!

I feel someone rush by me heading toward the bed. 'Not the bed! The 'spirit' I start to cry out, but don't. Aunt Pauline jumps on the bed with Mother. "Mary Alice, Mary Alice, I'm here." The minute she jumps on the bed, the 'spirit' is gone, everything disappears.

All I see is Aunt Pauline holding Mamma.

Mother's eyes open, but a blank look is there. No response from her but Aunt Pauline is talking away as if Mother understands what she is saying.

Mother is not yet free. She will be not be with her Lord this night. But wonderful things are still to happen to validate this glorious and majestic five and one-half hours. This is God's work, giving us a little more time to prepare this wonderful and glorified soul to take her journey to her final home.

13

Wings

Pat and I left the room and went out into the hallway. I grabbed Pat by the arm, "Oh, Pat, did she have gold wings? Were they down to the floor?"

"No, but she had the most beautiful silver wings and they went down to her waist."

We ran out onto the front porch. I fell to my knees crying, tears were running freely down my face and landing on the floor. I was holding on to Pat's waist with my hands. "Oh, Pat, tell me, tell me once more how she looked? Tell me again about her wings." Questions, one behind the other, flowed from my mouth, not giving Pat time to respond.

Then she started talking. "She was beautiful! She was beautiful! She was young, Mary Joe, and so beautiful." Pat's eyes were filled with tears as she continued. "Her hair was dark, long and wavy. When she made her turn, toward the three figures, I could see that her hair was swept back and downward, laying on the nape of her neck. Her wings were down to her waist." As she was describing this, her hands made a circular motion from her shoulders to her waist. "They were beautiful shiny silver wings."

"Pat, you saw Mother on her way. Mother was on her way!"

All the time Pat was talking her eyes were looking upward, toward the Heaven where this grandeur of events had come from. "I don't know what happened to her 'spirit,' Mary Joe. When Aunt Pauline jumped on the bed the spirit disappeared. I hope the 'spirit' wasn't hurt. We've got to find it."

"Don't worry Pat her 'spirit' will remain, until her body dies. It is still with Mother."

"Oh, Mary Joe it was so beautiful. She was so beautiful and those wings so shiny."

I stood up, looked into Pat's eyes, we hugged, held each other close and cried softly. We stood there for a while just being close. Both realizing, what we had seen was truly a heavenly gift.

Pat and I went back into Mother's room. Aunt Pauline was lying there cradling Mother in her arms. "Let's sing," she said.

James, Pat, Carol and I stood around the bed and the five of us, each crying, sang, "Rock of Ages", "In the Garden", "The Lord's Prayer", and "Amazing Grace".

Afterwards, Pat, Carol and I left the room so Aunt Pauline could be with Mother for a while. James stayed in the room with both of them.

14

The Spirit

When Pat, Carol and I got into the living room we started to explain to each other what we had seen.

Carol said, "I saw little children behind Mom's head. They were jumping and peeking over the top of her pillow as if trying to see her face."

"Well, that's not what I was seeing," said Pat.

"I'll tell you what we should do. Let's go into separate rooms and draw what we saw. Now don't try to be an artist, which none of us are, and then we'll come back and compare our drawings," I suggested.

Five minutes later the three of us sat down in the dining room and together we placed our drawings on the table.

I looked at Pat's paper. There was a square with a face in it. I jumped from my chair and yelled, "I saw that face. I saw it two times. Once when it went behind you and then appeared in front of your chest. And the second time, when it left the bed and traveled up James's arm and stopped at his heart.

Pat sat there with her mouth open looking at my paper and was pointing with her finger to the face in a square that I had drawn. She was trying to talk at the same time I was talking, "Look, look at this! This right here is what I saw!"

Then Pat pointed to some of her drawings, "See, this is the misty haze I saw over Mamma. And this was when you got up from the chair and came down to the foot of the bed after I told you there were two figures behind you. It was like a spotlight shining down on that chair. I mean a spotlight!!"

I started to explain about my drawing of the bed, "All behind the bed was the whitest white I had ever seen and there were gold streaks behind and over the bed. There were nine times I couldn't see Mother because of all this activity going on above her but below me; there were streaks and rays of gold and crystal clear light shooting in all directions. Between the rays were round objects like the top of people's heads. There was white light completely around Pat who was sitting next to the bed."

"I saw bright white light but most of the bed was surrounded by silver and gray-like lights. There was white and gold light behind Mamma. And there was white light around her head," Pat said. "Also see this chair, behind it is the three figures that I saw coming for Mamma. This one is Mamma, leaving; see her wings. Oh, she was beautiful..." Pat continued, "When I first started seeing something it was like little balls of light. Like a flash it appeared and was gone as fast."

Pat then pointed to the drawing of a face. "I could see this face located above Mamma's; I could also see through it, to Mamma. The shaded area was like a shadow on the face. I knew without a doubt that it was the face of Mamma's spirit.

We had not described to one another what we had seen and since we had referred to it mostly as simply "The Spirit" or "IT" during the five and one half hours the drawings we produced let each of us know that we had indeed had similar experiences...

Mary Joe's drawings of her experiences with
Mother's spirit.

Drawn around 12MN. Jan. 18, 1990

Spirit left or right
mother

mother

Face

Went behind Pat

white
square

Dark Hair
Mouth, Nose
and Eyes

Shape of
mouth
Changed
Shapes

White Light

Gold

White Light
Around Pat

PAT

white light

Gold

Bed
I couldn't see
mother on bed.
What
are the round objects?

Pat's drawings of her experiences with
Mother's spirit.

Carol's drawings of her experiences with Mother's spirit.

James crying with spirit shooting into his chest.

We then returned to Mother's room. Even though I knew Mother probably didn't know what I was saying, I told her, "I love you Mother."

I then left the room to sleep on a pallet in the living room. Before falling off to sleep I thought back on those five and one half hours and I knew that my life would be forever changed. The events of what I saw and what my sisters told me they saw would have to be shared with all peoples of this planet. Through help and guidance from the Higher Being I will not fail. Later Pat told me that she, Aunt Pauline and James sat and talked for a while in Mother's room Then Pat said, "I'm going to sit here with Mamma tonight."

"No need for you to stay up Pat. Why don't you lay down? Aunt Pauline and I are going to sit here with Mom," said James.

"Okay, but if y'all want to go to sleep, wake me up," Pat told them before she drifted off to sleep.

15

Time to Go

My eyes opened and I was struck with fear that something was wrong in Mother's bedroom. I had gone to sleep, on a pallet, in the living room about twelve thirty. Aunt Pauline wanted to stay in Mother's room that night so I agreed to sleep in another room. It was getting pretty crowded in that little room with all the people wanting to be near Mother. I jumped up and ran down the hall and into her room. Everyone was asleep. Aunt Pauline was bent over and her head resting on the bed, asleep. There Mother laid, her eyes open. I walked over to the bed and looked down at her. Mother's breathing was shallow and very slow and she was gulping for air. She was still stiff and rigid, and her whole body extremely cold. Her head was tilted toward me.

"My precious baby. You were all alone, but I'm here now," I said. As I climbed onto the bed Mother coughed, the odor coming from her mouth was putrid. I felt like I could vomit, but I took her in my arms and settled down into the bed. I carefully cradled her head onto my chest. I ran my hand lovingly over every inch of her face and rested it on her arm. "I love you, Mother," I said over and over again.

It felt wonderful to lay there beside Mother and be close. I held her little, stiff and cold, body next to me. I had a fleeting thought of placing Mother's face against my chest, blocking her from being able to breathe and it would all be over for this loving soul. In my heart I wanted to help her end this suffering but in my head I knew I couldn't. How much more time will I have with her? I knew it wouldn't be long.

I thought about those wonderful, five and one half hours that we had experienced earlier that night. "Mother, it was beautiful to be able to see where you're going. What a wonderful gift you and God gave to Pat, Carol and I tonight. I do know now, without a doubt, there is Life after Death. I knew this through, my faith, but now I have seen. It is so hard to let you go, but I know that for your spirit to leave us we must let your body go. Oh, Mother, how easy it is to say those words but so hard to abide by them. I know it is selfish for me to want to keep you here but your physical body is what I have known for all these years. It will be so lonesome without you. I can't even imagine my life going on, but I know God will comfort me through this crisis. But oh, Mother I want you to stay! I will miss you. I don't know whether you know what I'm saying to you, but if not, maybe you know that someone who loves you more than life itself is holding you, oh, so close." I cried myself softly to sleep.

Through the night I awoke several times, and on one of those occasions, I could feel the heat generating from Mother's body. She was no longer stiff, her body was now very limber, and her breathing was no longer gulping for air but was deep and even. I could not believe it! What was keeping her alive, was it the love and energy from us, her children. I drifted back off to sleep.

I felt a hand on my arm. I opened my eyes to see Pat leaning over Mother and her face close to mine. "Mary Joe, how is Mamma's heart?"

"I don't know, Pat, but look at her breathing, her respirations are better than mine. Feel her, she is warm and limber."

Pat felt her. "Mamma, what are you holding on for?" Pat said.

I told Pat about, my thoughts of, holding Mother's face to my chest and ending it for her.

"Oh, Mary Joe, you remember when the nurse was telling us about how to give the Roxanall under Mamma's tongue, to keep her relaxed. And I asked her, 'What if we give too much?' She said that Mamma would just go to sleep and not wake up. She would just die. Well, there was a time when Mamma was real restless and it was my turn to give the Roxanall. I went over and opened the bottle and put the medicine dropper in and suctioned up the medicine, filling the whole dropper. I thought this would put Mamma to sleep and she probably wouldn't wake up again. But I couldn't do it Mary Joe. I squirted it all out except for the 1\2 cc like the nurse had told us. It is so hard to see her in pain and her life like this. She was always such an active person. But I still want her as long as I can have her. Oh, Mary Joe, we got to let Mamma go. What is holding her here?"

"I don't know, Pat. I don't know. But I guess, maybe we are."

Within the hour the rest of the family was awake. Mother hadn't eaten or drank anything for a week. Will this be her last day of life? At this point, I don't believe any of us would attempt to make that prediction.

The nurse aide was due to come at ten o'clock to bathe Mother. The time came and went and the nurse aide hadn't arrived so Carol phoned Allcare Agency to see if she was still coming.

I got into the shower to freshen up. Pat came into the bathroom. "The nurse aide is sick and won't be here. The agency said they might be able to find someone else." There was a pause from Pat then she continued, "Mary Joe, why don't we bathe Mamma ourselves."

"That is fine with me," I responded.

By the time I got through bathing and getting dressed, Pat had a pan of warm water, lotion soap, a towel and wash cloth on the table by Mother's bed.

We began bathing Mother, starting at her face and head and working down to her legs and feet. We washed every inch of her body. Aunt Pauline was getting the bed linens together while we finished Mother's bath.

"Mother loves Oil of Olay," I told Pat. "Let's put it on her body." As we rubbed her lovingly with the lotion, we were both crying. "It's like they prepared the Lord after he was crucified," I said aloud and looked up at Pat. She looked into my eyes and sobbed openly. No other words needed to be spoken.

When we had finished I ran my hands across Mother's face, arms, chest, legs and feet. Her body felt like velvet, it was so smooth and warm. We changed her bed and placed her on her right side. What an experience we have had, the preparation of Mother to leave this world. One of many treasured memories from this week for me to remember about her.

Mother had lost so much weight and her mouth was so drawn inward, her lips were almost touching the back of her throat. It was as if something had sucked everything out of her. No matter, though, this was still my beautiful mother.

Pat said, "Mary Joe I'm so worried about what happened to Mamma's 'spirit' last night. I haven't seen it since Aunt Pauline jumped on the bed with Mamma."

"Don't worry, Pat. The 'spirit' will be with Mother until she draws in her last breathe of life. It must remain until the body lets it go."

"I hope so. I just hope that the spirit wasn't hurt or frightened when Aunt Pauline ran into Mamma's room and jumped on the bed and put her arms around Mamma. I know that Mamma wouldn't be here now if that hadn't happened. Oh, Mary Joe, it was so beautiful to see Mamma's spirit leaving. And then the little 'spirit' didn't get to go." Pat began to cry.

"I know, Pat, but maybe it was meant for Aunt Pauline to be able to talk one more time to Mother, while she was still alive. You know, sometimes there is unfinished business to take care of, even if there is only one person doing the talking. But look at it this way, if it had finished last night we wouldn't have had this glorious time bathing and preparing Mother for her journey, to meet her God."

Later in the afternoon, I was standing at the foot of Mother's bed and I noticed a movement above her body. Then the 'spirit' moved to the left of Mother's body. The 'spirit' is here! I didn't say anything to anyone. I wanted to just let the 'spirit' lie there in peace, above Mother. It was waiting for its time to go. It was waiting for Mother to pass on. We had received our gift last night that of watching her 'spirit' for five and one-half hours. Mother needed to receive her gift, hopefully, today that of Eternal Life!

16

Blood Red Sky

James had come to Carol's house on Monday morning January 15 without bringing any additional clothes. He also needed to go by his office, which was located between Carol's house and his, and check to see if he needed to take care of any business before the weekend. James left about three o'clock.

So much had gone on throughout the week, in that room, but life was also going on outside the room. Natalie had used my car to go to the bank on Wednesday to take care of a deposit for me and had locked the keys, the only set, in my car. It was Friday and I needed to get the car out of the banks parking lot. I called AAA and made arrangements for someone to meet me at six o'clock in the parking lot to help me get my car keys.

I called Pat into Mother's room. "Pat, I'm going to leave sometime between five and five-thirty, to go by my house and then go meet the person that can get the keys out of my locked car. I hate that I have to leave. I've been here since Sunday night. If Mother dies while I'm gone, it wasn't meant for me to be by her side when she leaves. Pat, if it really looks like she's going, please tell her, that I love her. Also, Pat, don't worry about the 'spirit.' I saw it over Mother earlier today."

"You did? Why didn't you tell me at the time?"

"Because it's time to let Mother go. And knowing the experience we had last night I knew it was enough to fill our hearts for the rest of our lives."

Natalie came by to pick me up to go get my car. Before leaving I went to Mother and bent over and gave her a kiss. "I love you, Mother." Her eyes were closed and I don't know whether she heard me or not, but that's okay.

We went by my house and picked up a few personal items, then left to get my car. We got to the parking lot at six o'clock. We got out of her car, as the weather was quite nice for this time of the year. We stood there in the lot talking. Natalie suddenly looked up into the sky toward the west.

She said, "Would you look at that sunset." The sun had already set but the reflection of the sun hitting the clouds created a sky that was blood red. It was the most striking sunset that I had ever seen. We stood there looking up for the longest time until the AAA representative arrived and opened up the car.

Since I was only a one mile from my son James house, I decided to go by there before I went back to Carol's. I knew my grandchildren, Shannon and Christopher, were visiting their dad and it had been several months since I last saw them. Also, it had been three weeks since I had seen my granddaughter Starr who lived with her dad. I walked to the door and knocked. James opened the door, looked into my eyes and said, "Grandma, is gone. Sue just called me, hoping you might be over here." I fell into James' arms and cried. Shannon, four years old, and Starr, ten years old, came over to me and both said, "I'm so sorry you're sad." Then they left the room, only to return within minutes. They handed me a folded piece of paper, and on the outside they had addressed it: to Meme, to Gram, from Shannon and Starr. I unfolded the paper and on the inside they had taken crayons and put streaks of seven different colors on the page, with the words, "I am sorry Meme." The colors tore at my heart. These precious children had put the colors of the rainbow on that page. The rainbow, a sign of the covenant that God made with man.

I met Natalie back at my house and we drove together back to Carol's. "You know, Natalie, I want to live as long as I can, but what I saw last night in Mother's room, I know without a doubt, where I'm going when I die; Mother will be waiting there for me when I leave this life to begin another, and so will all my relatives and friends that have gone, before me.

I walked into the house and went directly back to Mother's room. Pat and Carol were there. They had Mother lying on her back, eyes closed and her mouth closed. The bedding was straightened around her and they had placed her arms down at her sides. Pat and Carol had Mother looking so nice. It looked like she was asleep. I went to the bed and laid my body across her's and cried. "Mother, oh Mother I love you so. Why, why did this have to happen?" Pat and Carol left the room. "I hate that Dr. Matson. He couldn't take time to see if something was wrong, even though we told him you were no better. I blame him for letting the cancer grow for nine months before Dr. Thomas discovered it in October. Now I don't have a mamma." I stayed in the room with Mother for a while longer; then I left the bedroom and went into the living room where Pat, Carol and James were sitting.

Carol said that the nurse had been called to let her know Mother had died and when we were ready for her to come over to pronounce Mother dead just give her a phone call. It was close to eight o'clock and we all had time alone with Mother, so Carol made the phone call to the nurse. She lived in the general area of Mesquite, where Carol's home was located so she was there within minutes. Even though Mother had passed away well over an hour ago the nurse had to pronounce her dead at eight twenty when she listened for a heartbeat and did not hear one. She talked to Carol and Pat about what time Mother actually died. They said Mother died at about six-thirty-eight. That was about the time I was looking up into the sky at the blood red sunset.

The nurse then picked up the bottle of Roxanall and had Carol go with her into the bathroom and she poured the liquid into the sink, turned on the water and washed it down the drain.

It was time to phone the funeral home to come and get Mother's body.

Two men arrived from the funeral home. They came in and the nurse gave them all the information they needed before they could remove Mother's body from the house. Then they brought in a stretcher and went down the hallway. We were standing there looking at them. One of the men said, "I don't believe the stretcher will fit into the room. We need to carry her out here to the stretcher. I will go in and wrap Mrs. Davidson in the sheet."

James was standing near the stretcher and he said, "You can go in and put the sheet around Mother but her children will carry her out of that room." The man from the funeral home went in and came back out to say that she was ready.

We walked into the room; it would be the last time that we would go into the room and see Mother lying in the bed. Her face was left uncovered. I went to the head of the bed; James was next to me, then Carol and Pat. We were all crying uncontrollably. Tears were streaming down my face and, at times, I couldn't see Mother as my eyes were so filled with tears. I placed my hands and arms under Mother's head and neck. Pat, Carol on either side and James at her feet. When we were ready, we counted to three and lifted her gently and lovingly up off the bed. Then we carried Mother, feet first out the door, walked down beside the stretcher and placed Mother on it. We had taken Mother home from the hospital and put her in that room where she died with dignity, on January 19, 1990 at six-thirty-eight and we, her children, brought her out of that room with dignity.

The men pushed the stretcher into the living room. We asked them to give us a few minutes with Mother. We stood around Mother and openly cried, our hearts breaking, over the loss of this wonderful woman. I could never have asked for a better mother. I had the best. Even though we were still crying we quoted the Lords prayer:

Psalms 23.1-6
The Lord is my shepherd; I shall not want.
He maketh me to lie down in green pastures:
He leadeth me beside the still waters.
He restoreth my soul: He leadeth me in paths of righteous-
ness for his name's sake.
Yea, though I walk through the valley of the shadow of
death, I will fear no evil: for thou art with me; thy rod and thy
staff, they comfort me.
Thou preparest a table before me in the presence of mine
enemies: thou anointest my head with oil; my cup runneth over.
Surely goodness and mercy shall follow me all the days of
my life; and I will dwell in the house of the Lord forever.

And I thought, 'How true, how true. For I know without any reservation that Mother is, right now, dwelling with her, Lord.'

The men from the funeral home then took Mother's body out of the house at about ten o'clock. The house all of a sudden felt so empty.

Dwight wanted to know if we wanted to eat. He had cooked dinner earlier but didn't think we would want to eat until the funeral home came for Mother. I put the first bite into my mouth but I couldn't swallow the food. Pat was sitting beside me. She jumped up from the couch and ran down the hall crying and screaming, "Mamma! Mamma!" Her husband went after her. "Jack, I don't know what I'll do without my mamma."

I told Carol I was going to go on home. I hadn't been home for five nights. It felt good to lie down on my own bed but the memories of things I did with Mother rushed through my mind and it was impossible to go to sleep. I cried softly until I fell asleep.

17

Have a Wonderful Journey

Saturday morning I left home to meet James, Pat and Carol at Restland Memorial Park to make the funeral arrangements. Our appointment was for one o'clock. We were ushered into the office. The Director was at his desk and had Mother's file on the desk in front on him. James and I sat across from him. Carol and Pat sat on a couch positioned near the desk. We knew Mother had bought two grave plots and a funeral program back in 1971.

The Director let us know the last payment of twenty-two dollars was due. I couldn't believe it, the last payment. We were told the only remaining cost would be: flowers, newspaper notice, concrete vault, opening and closing of the grave, and the gravesite name marker.

Other than these items, this caring woman had once again showed the loving concern she had for us, her children, by making all these critical decisions nineteen years ago. She had picked all the colors, from the casket to the interior of it. She had written in the plan that she wanted her eye glasses in her hands, as if to have taken them off, for a moment, to rest her eyes and had fallen asleep.

Then he asked us, "What do you want us to do with her jewelry, her necklace."

"She didn't have a necklace on," I said.

"This cross, she had with her." And he pulled, out of the file, a Xerox copy of the cross. We all laughed and cried at the same time. We now knew that the cross was somewhere on Mother, when she left Carol's house going to the funeral home. She had not gone alone. Throughout that whole week we were with Mother, each one of us had placed or pushed the cross onto her chest, as she lay in the bed. Our finger prints on the cross had accompanied her. We asked the Director where they found it. He wasn't able to give an answer to us. I know that we couldn't find the cross on Friday afternoon when we discovered it was missing. We looked on the bed, under the sheets and looked on every inch of Mother's body. And I mean every inch. We couldn't find it. Now there it was. It had been on Mother but where? Then we knew, it was meant for us to make this trip with Mother, if not physically, then through our love in making sure the cross was always lying on Mother's chest near her heart.

The Director told us Mother would be ready for us to see around five o'clock. It was almost four, so we decided to go over to the floral shop and order a family casket spray. We ordered red roses and an arrangement of pink roses and baby's breath to be wrapped around the top and bottom of a picture of Mother that was going to be at the head of her casket. The picture was of Mother, when she was twenty years old. We also went ahead and ordered the flowers from the Grandchildren and Great-Grandchildren.

The cross and form from the funeral parlor.

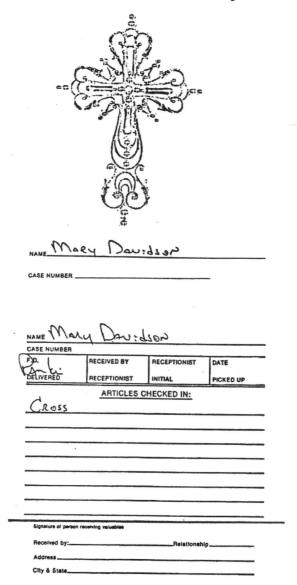

NAME Mary Davidson

CASE NUMBER

NAME Mary Davidson

CASE NUMBER

F.D. DELIVERED	RECEIVED BY	RECEPTIONIST	DATE
	RECEPTIONIST	INITIAL	PICKED UP

ARTICLES CHECKED IN:

Cross

Signature of person receiving valuables

Received by:_____Relationship_____

Address_____

City & State_____

The time had come for us to go into the viewing room. We walked in and there was my precious mother.

James, Pat, Carol and I walked over to the casket and looked down at Mother. When the mortician prepares the body he or she will not be able to make the person exactly like you remember them. Close but not exact. I thought they did a good job on Mother but Carol had wanted less filling in the jaws and mouth, as Mother never was one to wear her false teeth. Pat and James never commented one way or the other. Mother didn't wear lipstick so they removed it from her lips and applied a very soft gloss to them.

Mother looked like she was sleeping. She had her eye glasses lying on her chest and was holding the little white Bible and the cross that she had held close to herself, for the last two months of her life. The turban Pat had given to her for Christmas was on her head and made her look majestic. The pink bed jacket matched the pajamas perfectly. The interior of the casket matched her pink outfit perfectly. She had made a great choice, she looked so natural.

Carol asked if they still burnt candles in holder stands near the casket. The Director informed her it was usually done if the person was Catholic. She then said that Dad had them positioned at the head and foot of his casket and that he wasn't Catholic. She let him know the reason she wanted to know was she burns those candles for a few minutes every Christmas, in memory of Dad. She had hoped to have candles from Mother's funeral too.

Then I noticed that the crystal stone that I had taped to the little heart pillow, that Natalie had given to Mother, for Christmas, was missing. I had given Mother the crystal and had placed it in her pillow cases ever since she started her treatments. I asked where the crystal was. The Director looked in the casket around where the little pillow was placed but was unable to find it. He left to see if it was among other personal things of Mother's. Pat said, "Mary Joe, I believe I have a crystal here in my purse." She looked, then emptied the contents out onto the table. There it was. She handed it to me. I was taping it to the pillow when the Director came in carrying a box with Mother's items in it. Sure enough, there was the crystal, I picked it up out of the box and taped it to the pillow. I handed Pat's crystal back to her. She said, "Can't my crystal go with Mother too?"

"Sure it can, Pat." Pat handed it to me and I walked over and laid it beside Mother's right leg. We both carried crystals in the belief that crystals would add positive energy to our lives.

The Director told us that the room that Mother was in actually was two rooms, but since they didn't need the extra room, they had opened up the folding doors to allow us to have more space. There were several tables with lamps, a couple of chairs and a small couch. This was quite comfortable for those wanting to visit Mother.

We all went back to Carol's house. When we arrived Liz and Marie were there. Marie said she wanted to talk privately to us. We went into the room where we had taken care of Mother for all those three months. Pat and I sat on the couch, while Carol sat on the bed. Marie stood in front of us. "I went to bed, last night, and of course my thoughts were of you girls and the loss of your mother. I had a dream and I wanted to tell you what I dreamed. "There were three women in a hallway and a room with blue carpet. The three women were crying and saying, "We don't have our crystal, we can't get in." One of the women came to me, and Carol I knew it was you because the woman worn her hair like you. She said, "I don't have the crystal lantern. I don't have the crystal lantern." I turned to this woman and gave her a crystal lantern. But the other two women kept saying, "But we don't have our crystal, we can't get in." I woke up and on the night stand was my crystal lantern like the one I saw in my dream, so I knew that I must give it to you Carol. Also I knew that Mary Joe and Pat needed to have their crystal. She gave me a cut leaded crystal egg and gave Pat cut leaded crystal coasters. When Marie was through I said, "Now let me tell you what happened today." I told her what Carol had said to the Director, about the candles that had been placed at the head and foot of Dad's casket, and she was hoping to get the candles that would burn near Mother's casket. I then told her about the lost crystal from the pillow and about Pat giving me her's. Then the crystal was found, but Pat wanted her crystal to go with Mother, too, so I placed it by Mother's right leg, and I looked at Marie and said, "By the way, in the room where Mother's casket is, the carpet is blue.

The five of us remained in the room talking. Then I asked Pat to tell me what happened after I had left on Friday to go get the car.

"After you left Carol and I were in the room talking. As it began to get dark I got up off the couch and went over to the foot of the bed and looked at Mamma's body, wondering what had happen to the Spirit. I know you told me you had seen it but I had to try and satisfy myself that the Spirit was still there. All of a sudden I saw the spirit. About that time Carol turned on a small lamp on the dresser. Then as soon as she turned it on she said, 'No I'm not going to leave it on, because the neighbors can see in.' She turned the lamp off. There, the Spirit was, right there, just a little bit above Mother, lying on its side. I just went, 'Aaah!!' I looked at Carol and I walked out of the room. Carol came out and said, 'Did you see it? Did you see it?'

"'Yes,' I replied.

"'I did too,' echoed Carol. About that time the phone rang and I went to answer it. It was James David, he wanted to know how Mamma was, I told him that her breathing was real shallow, real shallow and he said that he was on his way back over. While I was talking another call came through. It was the nurse, so I gave the phone to Carol. Just as Carol started talking to her, Sue who had been in Mamma's room with us stepped out of the room and said, 'Grandma's eyes are open.' I hurried back into the room and yelled for Carol to get back to Mamma's room. She ran in still talking to the nurse on the phone. She told the nurse, 'Mom is dying now. She is breathing like a little fish out of water.' But Mamma's eyes were not wide open like she was scared or anything. Her eyes were glassy and set, she was just staring. It was a soft look, you know, in her eyes. Aunt Pauline wanted to get to Mamma, so bad, but Carol and I said, 'Let her go. Let her go, Aunt Pauline.'

"We were hollering that we loved her. Then I said, 'Mamma I love you... Mary Joe loves you... Carol loves you... James loves you... Richard, Jimmy, Billy, Sue, Jennifer, Brett, Ginger, Deanna, Brian, Erin and all your Great-Grandchildren love you.'

'Mother have a wonderful journey.'

"She took about three or four more breaths. Carol picked up the stethoscope and walked over to Mamma and listened for a heartbeat. Carol looked at me and shook her head, 'she's gone,' and we started crying."

"We straightened Mamma up in bed. Carol had told the nurse that we would call her when we were ready. You know, we just wanted more time with her, we didn't want to give her up right then. We knew that you and James would need your time, with Mamma."

"While we sat in the bedroom waiting for you and James to come back, Carol told me what she had seen right after she turned off the light in Mamma's room. 'Pat, there were heads of people all over the bed. They were at Mom's chest, arms, stomach, knees and hips. They were everywhere on the bed. The people were waiting for Mom, Pat!'

"I heard a car drive up so I left the bedroom and went into the living room. James came running into the house. He looked at Sue and said, 'Grandma, Grandma.' Then he looked at me, 'Mamma, Mamma.' I told him that she was gone. He ran down the hall and into her room. 'I wanted to be here. I wanted to be here. I was here for four days. I was here for four days.' I told him that if it was meant for him to be here he would have. James was devastated."

I looked at Pat after she got through telling me all that had happened while I was gone. "Well, Pat, Mother was right when she told you two years ago, you would be with her when she died. You and Carol were the ones chosen, to send Mother off on her next life's journey. I feel bad about not being here when Mother passed on, but I believe what is meant to be, will be. I hope James understands that to. It was not meant for either of us to be here, at that time."

18

Her Life in Pictures

I left Carol's house about nine o'clock. When I got home I told Natalie all we had done that day and that the picture of Mother when she was young was going to be placed at the head of the casket.

She said, "It's nice to have the picture of your Mother when she was young. Since her friends at the high rise only knew her in her senior years, wouldn't it be nice to have your Mother's life, in pictures, displayed in the viewing room."

"That would be great, Natalie. I have a lot of pictures of Mother taken over the years." I went into my closet and pulled out albums and boxes of pictures.

Now would come the job of finding the pictures to be used. Natalie had an assortment of portfolios to put the pictures in that I picked out. I was sad about Mother's death, but there was an air of excitement, putting together the story of Mother's life in pictures. I found pictures of her, from the time she was in her twenties until now. Natalie said she would help me since it was so late. She mentioned it would be nice to create an every-ten-year account of Mother's life in pictures. I even had a newspaper article written back in 1972 about our trip to Hawaii with a picture of Mother and Don Ho taken, when we attended the Don Ho Luau. Natalie took all the pictures and put together the display. We had worked through most of the night to get it ready to take and set up in the viewing room. I appreciated what Natalie had suggested and that she put together this picture tribute to Mother. You could tell the results was the work of a professional photographer.

Tired, I fell quickly to sleep.

Sunday morning I awoke around eight o'clock. I wanted to get to the funeral home and get the pictures arranged before noon. I took a shower and dressed. I was ready to go. I needed to eat breakfast before I left but food was not something I had been able to deal with since Mother's last week of life and her death. Maybe it was because I knew Mother hadn't eaten anything that week, it was like I shouldn't eat either. I don't know, but it was hard for me to swallow the food in my mouth.

We arrived at the funeral home and, since we had use of the extra room there was plenty of space to put the pictures on display. I've never attended a funeral where there was a pictorial story about the deceased. It was different and it was certainly a wonderful tribute to this remarkable woman.

I stayed in the room with Mother so I could see and talk to her friends when they came to pay their respect. I could tell it was hard on these women when they viewed Mother's body. Pat or Carol were in and out of the room throughout the day, and when no one else was in the room it gave me time to just be with Mother.

Early in the afternoon my son, James arrived with his family. Two of my grandchildren went over to Mother's casket to look at her. I started to pick up Shannon, my four year old granddaughter, to take her over to see her Grandma Davidson, as she called Mother, but James said not to. I didn't say anything but I felt that we all need to experience closure.

I left the funeral home about five o'clock, and went by Carol's for dinner. Carol had told James and me to come by her house, as her neighbors had brought food over during the day for the family. At a time like this, most people can depend on their neighbors. I have never been able to thank them personally, but if they read this book about this wonderful woman, I want to here and now say, "Thank you for what you did, to make things easier, for the Mary Alice Davidson family, on January 20-22, 1990."

Pat, Jack and Brian David came over to my house on Sunday evening to spend the night. Mother's brothers and sisters began to arrive from Arkansas on Sunday. Several hotel rooms had been reserved for them in a hotel up the street from Carol's house. Also several family members were going to stay at Carol's.

I didn't sleep most of the night. I cried a lot knowing that when the sun went down tomorrow it would all be over and our lives would go on. But it would go on without me being able to see my mother ever again.

Mary Alice Davidson

DAVIDSON

Mary Alice, age 77, died January 19, 1990 at the home of her daughter. Born August 13, 1912 in London AR. She moved to Dallas, TX in 1956 and lived for many years in the Mesquite area. She was a former resident of Lakeland Manor in Dallas where she lived 10 years prior to her illness. Beloved, mother of Mary Joe Risher, Mesquite, James David Davidson, Irving, Patricia Ann Bolton, of Texas City, Carol Jean Mrydahl, Mesquite; sons-in-law, Dwight Mrydahl and Jack C. Bolton, Sr.; grandchildren, Deanna and (Kenny), Ginger, Sue and (John); great-grandchildren, Justin, Nicholas and Daniel; Christopher, Starr and Shannon; Shaun, Brittany and Tiffany; Erin; brothers, Cecil (Christell) and Joe Jr. (Lorene) Petray, Malvern, AR; sisters, Aline Baker, Dardanelle, AR, Pauline Reddell, W. Richland, WA; Joan Ballard, Arkadelphia, AR; sister-in-law, Alice Petray, Malvern, AR; host of nieces, nephews and friends. Services 2:00 P.M. Monday, RESTLAND MEMORIAL CHAPEL. Interment Restland Memorial Park. Pallbearers will be the grandchildren: James and Richard Risher, Bill and Jennifer Myrdahl, Britt Davidson and Brian Bolton.

RESTLAND
Greenville Ave. at Restland Rd.
236-7111

19

Black Eyed Peas

Monday morning had arrived I got up and went into the kitchen to start breakfast. I moved routinely not making conversation with anyone. Today would be the last time I would have to touch or kiss the physical body of my beloved mother. When I thought of this I would get choked up.

I went into the pantry to get a box of cereal for Brian and directly in front of me, on a shelf, was a bag of Black-eyed peas. I chuckled as I picked up the bag and brought it back into the kitchen. I put the peas in a pan of water and let them cook while I got ready to go to Carol's. Arrangements had been made for the funeral home limousine to pick up the four of us there. When it was time to leave I went into the kitchen, poured the cooked peas into a jar and capped it. Now I was ready to go, jar and all.

At one o'clock the limousine arrived and we were on our way to Restland's Wildwood Chapel where the service was to be held.

I went into the chapel. There were flowers everywhere, throughout the room and all around the casket. I took the jar of black-eyed peas and placed it on one of the pedestals, behind a floral arrangement.

Later, just before the two o'clock service began, I was talking to Carol and several of Mother's friends from the Senior Citizen high-rise. Sue, Carol's daughter, came up to us and remarked, "Did any of you see that jar of peas on the pedestal, at the foot of Grandma's casket? I wonder who would do that."

"I did," I answered.

"You did?" was Sue's response.

"Yes. Many times, I have heard Mother say to people when they were talking about death or funerals, 'Rather than sending me flowers, you can bring me a bowl of Black-eyed peas.' The response would be, 'Black-eyed peas, you can't eat those peas.' And Mother's answer was always the same, 'I can eat those peas, as well as, I can smell those flowers.'"

We all broke into a low laughter.

The chaplain from the hospice program was asked if she would officiate at Mother's funeral. Carol had made arrangements several months ago with her friend, Father Luke. He had agreed, but death is not scheduled by appointment and when Mother died he was on vacation. The chaplain said she would be happy to perform the service.

The pallbearers would be five of Mother's grandsons, James, Richard, Britt, Bill, Brian and one of her granddaughters, Jennifer. She had held, loved and baby-sat each of those six grandchildren, when they were young. There they sat, all grown adults now. It was right that they should be the ones to carry her those last few feet to the gravesite.

The chaplain was talking about who Mary Alice Davidson was and those whose lives she had touched, family and friends. She continued, "One of Mary Alice's daughters, Pat has written two poems in tribute to her mother. Pat read these poems to her mother several years ago. A privilege, not all of us will have, that of knowing what will be read at our funeral."

TRIBUTE TO OUR MOTHER
From her children
Written by Patricia Bolton

God came and took you from us.
He holds your loving hands.
He wants to show you his world now,
A world that is so grand.

God must have said;
Mary come go with me,
I'll show you wonders you've never seen.
My Garden is a Paradise.
My Streams are crystal clear.
There will be more love in Heaven,
Now that you are here.
I will walk beside you,
Every step of the way.
We will walk and talk together,
For MARY this is your day

So take my hand,
It is time for us to go.
I will take care of you now,
FOR I LOVE YOU SO.

The song "In the Garden" was sung at the end of the poem.

The selection, "In the Garden", "Precious Memories", "Old Rugged Cross", "Rock of Ages", and "Amazing Grace", were songs Mother had loved and indicated she would like to be played or sung at her funeral.

The chaplain continued with the tribute in poem.

MOTHER it is time for us to say good-bye.
It is time to let you go.
Our grief we must try to endure
For we also loved you so.

Words cannot express,
The way we feel today.
Our hearts feel like they are broken,
Our MOTHER has gone away.
MOTHER was a warm, a tender, a loving and caring person.
Helping others was her goal.
All her friends will miss her,
For they also loved her so.
You are away,
Yet ever so near,
Your voice, your smile will be everywhere,
For us just a memory away.

Although you will no longer be seen,
By family or by friends,
You will live, because you were dearly loved,
AND LOVE CAN NEVER END.

The words still pounding within my heart as "Precious Memories" is being sung. 'Oh, how strong are those memories I hold so dear of my mother. There will be no future memories to remember, only past memories and they flood my head with happiness and joy. I will be able to recall these treasured memories, at any given time, from now on for the rest of my life. Oh, those precious memories.'

The service was over, it was time to go to the gravesite, but one last look at Mother. Mother! Mother! My legs could hardly hold me up for me to walk to the casket. I know James, Pat and

Carol were having their own emotions to deal with. We all had to make the final trip to say good-bye. I stood by the casket. I looked down, reached out and touched Mother's hands and then her face. Then I bent over and kissed her lips. My last contact with this woman who had given me life.

We got into the family limousine and sat there while we watched Mother's grandchildren carry her casket and place it in the hearse. Now we would follow this remarkable woman in her lifetime, for the last time! As the limousine we were in came to a stop the casket was being lifted out of the hearse by her grandchildren. I watched my own two sons, James and Richard, and my heart cried for them. My thoughts went back to the many times Mother had been around them and had wanted them to spend the weekends with her. The memories of the four years that we lived with Mother, after their father and I were divorced. I can see Mother now, carrying three year old Richard, over to the babysitter, as we got ready to leave for work, in the mornings. The holidays when Richard would call and tell Mother, "Grandma, I want to put my order in for two pecan pies and two pumpkin pies." She was a fantastic cook and we all knew it. She was with me at the hospital when James was born and she was with me when I brought him home. James was her first grandchild and both Mother and Dad spent a lot of time with him in his childhood years. Then my eyes went to Jennifer. When we were talking about who would be the pallbearers and named the grandsons, we came up with five. Someone mentioned another male member of the family, but he was not a grandchild. I said, "Why don't we ask Jennifer if she would like to be a pallbearer? After all, who says a pallbearer has to be a male. Mother carried her around when she was a baby just like she did the boys." Mother loved her grandchildren and they loved and respected her, the Matriarch.

We got out and walked to the gravesite. The chaplain conducted a short service and it was time for us to go. Go! Leave!

It was so hard to turn and walk away from Mother but we had to. The casket had to be lowered and covered and the funeral home personnel wouldn't do that while we are still there.

The limousine took us back to Carol's house. We walked into the house, it was full of people who had known Mother. Carol and Mother's neighbors had brought food over to the house, while we were at the funeral. There was food in the dining room, kitchen and den. There was enough food to feed the whole residential block. It all looked good but, right then, I don't think I could have eaten anything.

Mother's brothers, sister-in-laws, sister and nephew needed to get started on their trip back to Arkansas. We all went out into the front yard. We were all saying our good-byes. Natalie asked me if I wanted her to take a picture of the whole family before they left. I told everyone it was picture taking time. We all grouped around. The picture was taken. Uncle Cecil said, "You all keep in touch with us." as he got into the car.

After they left, Natalie turned to me and said she wanted to take a picture of the four of us.

As we positioned ourselves for the picture, my thoughts went back to past years. At family get-togethers we always had a group picture taken just before we left Mother and Dad's, then headed home. Before Dad died there were the six of us in a picture. Before Mother died there were the five us in a picture.

We stood there, arms around each other's backs and the picture was taken of the four of us.

Afterwards, we stood in the front yard talking to each other. I turned and looked at James David, Patricia Ann and Carol Jean. I wondered, 'Who will be left for the picture of three?' And at this thought, my heart cried.

20

The Final Chapter

(Pat telling us in her own words)

Carol

Mary had moved to Washington State after Mother passed away. I started going to visit her regularly. It was so nice, because of my MS, to get away from the Texas heat.

I planned to visit Mary in October 2004 and work for her until after Christmas, but I wanted to go see our younger sister Carol in Yantis, Texas first. We had a nice visit, reminiscing and laughing a lot. Carol and I were close, I was 3 years older, and we did a lot of things together growing up. When I left Carols' she seemed healthy and happy. After our visit I headed off to see Mary in Washington State.

A few weeks later we got a phone message from Carol. She was letting us know she was at Parkland Hospital in Dallas having some tests run. She said that she hadn't been feeling well and thought she might have kidney stones.

It was Thanksgiving weekend and she would have to wait for the test results to come back, but she wanted to talk to us first. Mary returned Carol's call. As they talked their conversation changed, it sounded different, more intense. I asked Mary, "What's going on?" She handed me the phone. "What's wrong Carol?" She said, "Pat, it doesn't look good for me." "Oh Carol, don't say that. Nothing is going to happen to you. We have things to tell the world about what we experienced when mother was dying." I hung up the phone feeling worried about what they might find.

We were still waiting to hear back from Carol with her test results when she called me and said "Pat I had a dream about you last night. I saw myself at the bottom of some steps that went all the way to Heaven. A man with a long white gown was there, St. Peter I guess. I told him "I think I died and on my way to Heaven." He gave me a piece of chalk and told me for every step I took to write down every sin I had committed. After moving up several steps I saw you come running down past me. I yelled "Pat where are you going?" You answered back "for another piece of chalk". We laughed and she told me it was a joke our brother had shared with her. We had no idea how close to the truth it was.

Carol called us early the next morning to let us know the results were back, she had Pancreatic Cancer and was in stage 3 or 4 with little chance for recovery. It was devastating news.

We made a point of talking to her every day. I told Carol she could call any hour day or night, as many times as she wanted and she did. We talked and cried a lot during those calls, and I said how much I loved her and how I was going to miss her and what a joy it was to have her for my little sister.

I wanted to be with her, but knew I had to wait for at least 2 more weeks. I prayed to God every day to keep her alive until I could get there.

Finally I was able to fly to Dallas. James met me at the airport and we drove to Carol's about an hour and a half away. When we arrived I jumped out of the car and ran through the house straight to Carol's bedroom.

Carol looked as if she wasn't expecting me, but then a big sigh of relief came from her when she realized I was finally there to take care of her. A promise we made to each other after mothers death. I walked over to her and held her in my arms. She looked so thin and was very weak. Mary told me to call her as soon as I got there to let her know how Carol looked. I stepped outside to call. "Mary you better get here as soon as you can, Carol looks really bad." Mary said it would be at least a week before she could get there after Christmas.

Carol had her ups and downs, she was rushed back to the hospital on Christmas Eve but was able to return home again on Christmas Day. I called Mary and told her Carols' condition had worsened and she needed to get here right away. She said she would change her ticket to fly out on the 27th.

One of Carols' cows gave birth to a calf Christmas morning, I named her Christmas Carol, C.C. What a wonderful homecoming gift for Carol, as she loved her little herd of cows so much. Throughout the day she enjoyed seeing the new calf bounce around the field, watching it from her bedroom window.

Carol was resting peacefully that evening, so we moved into the den to watch the news about the devastating Tsunami in Indonesia. We had the TV on low as they talked about the death toll. All of a sudden we heard Carol from the other room, "here I am dying and wouldn't you know it, with all those people dying I guess I'm going to have to stand in line." We all laughed, that was Carol. She had high energy, always in a rush to get to where she was going, many times as she stood waiting impatiently in a line, she made a point of expressing herself loudly to anyone within earshot, and "wouldn't you know it I picked the wrong line."

Carol was going downhill fast and had to be taken back to Parkland Hospital on the 27th to have a stint put in her liver.

When Mary arrived she went directly to the hospital. She wanted to stay overnight with Carol after the surgery, so the rest of us headed back to Carol's house.

Mary told us about what happen in the hospital during the night. Carol started yelling out for Mary to help her. She kept saying "No, no I'm not ready, help me, Mary help me, I can't go yet, help me. Mary jumped on the bed and took Carol in her arms saying, "Its ok big sister's got you. I won't let them take you." Carol calmed down and finally fell asleep.

Carol was released the next day, she had made the decision not to stay in the hospital or receive any more treatments. She wanted to spend her last days in her own home with her family. Little did we know how few days we were going to have with her?

Carol had told James to stay close to her as he might see something or take a journey with her during her death. She hoped this would be similar to what we had experienced with Mother.

Over the next several days we made her as comfortable as we could, and took turns staying by her side. We played beautiful music which she loved listening to.

The evening of Jan 2nd Mary and Carol's daughter gave Carol a sponge bath and dressed her in a pretty pair of new pajamas Mary had bought for her. I was on the back porch looking through the window as they lovingly finished dressing her, I thought how beautiful she would look when her time came to meet her maker, Jesus, Mother and Daddy.

Carols' mouth was open almost like she was yawning but I could see a heat wave coming out her mouth, It was not like the mist that I had seen with mother but I knew what it was, her "Spirit".

At around 3:15 am most of the family was outside, sitting on the deck, when Mary called us to come in as Carol was nearing the end. We all together said, "We're here Carol. We're here." We stood there, Mary, James, and I watching our baby sister, who was only 59 years old, take her last breath and we knew she was immediately in her final home. On January 3, 2005 at 3:30 am the question was answered.

Who would be left for a picture of three?

James
James was not that close to the family after he got married. His job moved him and his family to several cities out of state.

At the time that mother found out she was terminal ill James had moved back to moved Dallas. He was a great help to Carol, Pat and me in taking care of mother until she died.

When I moved to Washington State I would always go back at Christmas to visit my sister, Pat, in Texas City Texas and she would visit me every year in the summer months.

In 2010 my brother James moved in with her and her husband, Jack. Shortly, after his move they found that Jack was terminally ill and within ten months Jack passed away.

James began to visit me, for six weeks at a time, and seemed to really enjoy being here on Lopez Island, as did Pat when she visited.

In 2011 on my yearly trip, to visit Pat and James at Christmas, we sat having breakfast and James said, "How would you like brother and sister to move to Lopez with you." I said, "That would be great. When are you thinking about the move?" He responded, "I would like to come up there in the spring and find us a place to live and we plan on moving in August." James came in May for 6 weeks, put a deposit on a rental and returned to back to Texas City.

Pat arrived on July 31 to get the house ready to move in. We shopped for cleaning items and groceries for them. I told Pat, "There is one more thing we need to do before James gets here. I need to get you both signed up with Airlift Northwest. Should you or James, have an emergency and need to get to a hospital, you will have to be flown off the island by helicopter." I made the call and signed them up. "Can you believe seventy nine dollar for insurance for both of you for one year." This would the best money they ever spent.

James arrived on August 10. I will never forget his first words to me when he got out of the car. "This is where I am going to finish it out."

In September Pat and I had to fly back to Texas City to pick up her two dogs and get her house ready to sell. We returned to Lopez a month later, driving back in Pat's car, it was packed to the roof with just a small space for her dogs to lay on top of the trunks in the back seat. It was a four day adventure and we made it without any problems. One thing that amazed me was the dogs. They learned quickly that when we stopped at a gas station it was only to get gas, so they would not try to get out. When we stopped at a rest area they seemed to know it was their time to get out of the car to do their business, eat and get a drink of water.

I was glad to finally get home as I had to get ready for a three day craft show in Lynden October 18th through 20th. We were at the show when I got a call from the EMT director on Lopez. She told me "Your brother James is being flown off the island, as we speak, to the Bellingham hospital. He has had a major stroke and he is not going to make it." I hung up the phone and told Natalie we needed to get packed up and get to the hospital right away.

I immediately called our sister Pat and told her what the EMT had told me, she was very upset. I said "I'll call you as soon as I get to the hospital." We were only 30 minutes away from hospital in Bellingham.

James was in the ICU when Natalie and I arrived at the hospital. I was able to speak with the doctor. He informed me, "Your brother had an aneurysm that ruptured causing him to be brain dead and he probably will not make it through the night. I called Pat to tell her the devastating news, and told her I would put the phone up to James' ear and she could tell him goodbye and whatever she wanted to say. At one point while she was talking to him we saw him give a small jerk as if he might have recognized her voice or what she might have said. James passed away at 3:30 am Sunday October 21, 2012 one month before his 74th birthday. Now there are two of us left, Pat and me.

"What does those two 3:30 am deaths mean Mary?" Pat said.

"All I can say Pat, for us, "The clock keeps ticking."

The Meeting Place

There was a knock at the door. I opened the door and standing there in front of me is my sister Carol and my brother James. Carol said, "Are you ready?" I didn't have time to respond to her before she said they would be around the corner waiting for me in a taxi. I watched them walk down the sidewalk and disappear around the corner.

I was very puzzled at what had just happened so I walked to the corner and looked around. I didn't see a taxi so I headed back inside the house.

There was a knock at the door again. I opened the door and standing there was the taxi driver. She said, "We are waiting for you. You need to come with me now or we are going to be late." I followed her around the corner to the taxi. I climbed in the front beside her and looked back to see Carol and James in the backseat.

We took off and after a short drive we pulled up to the departure level at the airport. The three of us got out and went inside to the ticket counter. I stood watching Carol put her bag on the scale and as she handed her ticket to the agent, she turned toward me and asked me, "Where are your bags? Where is your ticket?"

"I don't have any bags. I don't have a ticket," I answered.

Carol looked over at James and back at me, "I don't have the money for you a ticket."

Then James chimed in " Sister, you know, I don't have the money for you a ticket."

They turned got their boarding passes and left me standing there, watching them disappear around the corner.

My sister Carol passed away on January 3, 2005 and my brother James passed away on October 21, 2012.

Sometimes in the quiet of night in our dream time, those who have passed on and those who remain here have such a strong desire to see their loved ones that they reconnect together in a space that I like to call the 'meeting place.' I feel such peace when I am there, and I know that our time together can be repeated over and over again.

I am so glad I didn't have my bags packed and I didn't have a ticket. I truly believe my sister and my brother, wanted to take me back to heaven with them.

But, Carol or James didn't have money to buy me a ticket

I guess that old saying, 'You can't take it with you when you die' is so true.

21

Questions

To All My Readers

I felt like when I wrote Angel in Disguise: Bridging This World to the Other Side that it would be conclusion of the story, but I found that it was only the beginning. So many questions from myself and others have come into the light. I found myself wanting to let those readers know, as they may have the same questions. I believe over the period of time God has sent people into my life that I could receive the answers. I hope some of these answers I received from people along my path will give you answers to your questions.

Wings

In the drawings we made in chapter 14, Pat and Carol had both drawn wings on mother's spirit. We were amazed how similar, but different, our drawings were when we placed them on the table for first time. During our 5 ½ hour journey to the other side no description was ever said of what we were seeing. We just referred to 'It' or the 'Spirit'.

I had an opportunity to give a talk in a workshop, at a Spirituality Conference, in Los Angeles. After my talk Natalie and I wanted to go to see what, products, vendors had at the show. I opened the vendor catalog and looked down. "I need to go to that booth." She said, "What is there?" "I don't know but I've got to go there," I said. Natalie said she would meet me at the end of the aisle and I left to go the booth. I stood there. "What am I doing here?" I put my workshop papers down on the table just as a woman stood up from behind the table. She pointed to the papers, "I've got to go listen to that woman talk." I'm that woman and I've already talked." "Tell me about this," pointing to the angel on my paper. I told her about the journey and that Pat and Carol had seen wings on mother. This woman was standing in front of me crying, tears flowing down her face. "Mother was a wonderful woman," I said.

She looked at me, "You don't know." Then what she said validated the 'Wings' seen on mother. "Every once in a while an angel goes to God and says, I want to go to Earth and see what it is like to be a human being." Then she said, "Your mother was exactly what she was before she ever came. She was an angel." This wonderful woman who owns a large bookstore and restaurant on Highway 101, north of Los Angeles has given me just one more part to the addition of this book and its story.

Dallas Bookstore

This story is almost a continuation of the Wing story. I had gone to Dallas and happen to be in a metaphysical book store. I found myself in a conversation with the store owner and a woman that was there. We started talking about angels. I told them about meeting this woman in Los Angeles a month ago and what she told to me.

The young woman said, "What it must have been like to be raised by an angel." I didn't know. Then a voice within my soul said to me, "No you didn't know, that the woman who wiped away your tears, who sewed your formal for your prom, was one of my angels. Nor does anyone know that a homeless person might be one of my angels.

The young woman wanted to know about my mother. I said, "Mother came from a family of eight siblings. They were a poor family but happy and mother worked, picking cotton, in a bakery and was a waitress. She always gave her mother her money as did the others. Mother was kidnapped when she was sixteen. She fought the two young men off. They dropped her at a house and fled without harming her. Mother's family came for her and took her home.

At twenty-four she married my father on August 13, 1936. He was abusive to mother and after 33 years of marriage mother divorced dad, with her four children blessing."

The young woman looked at me, "Well, she sure found out what is was like to be a *'Human Being,'* but on so many different levels.

Psalm 91:4 God shall cover thee with his feathers and under his wings you may seek refuge.

Los Angeles TV Show

Pat and MarJoe

We were in Los Angeles to be interviewed on a TV show. Mary Joe and I were in the hotel room talking as we were getting ready to leave for the TV studio. I said to her, "I had the biggest smile on my face." She said, "What did you say?" I said, "I had a biggest smile on my face."

  She looked at me and said, "How do you know that?" And I responded, "I saw myself smiling." Then at that very moment, I realized that, 'my spirit,' had separated from my physical body and was moving around as I sat motionless in that chair. This was hard for me to acknowledge and even believe but it would have been the only way I could have seen myself smiling. I would have had to be standing directly in front of myself, sitting in the chair.

A Journey of a Lifetime

In this book you read about three sister's journey with their mother to the Other Side. I am sure as you finished reading this part of the book you had a question about their brother James. He was also in the room with his dying mother. Why didn't James get to go with his sisters on this journey? When all this started Mary had made the statement that she was seeing mother's spirit. James had made the comment, "All I see is mother body." I feel that he couldn't get a pass the physical and was not open to a miracle underway and happening in that room. We all were on a TV show in Houston to tell our story. The host of the show asked, "James you was in that room with your sisters. Did you get to take the journey? James answered, "No I did not. Debbie. I would have given anything in this world to see what my sister's say they saw. But, Debbie I thank God every day that I was in that and they were seeing something. I would look into their faces and not even know where they were. So during the evening one might say 'The spirit is beautiful.' And then nothing was said for quite a while. Then one of them might say 'the spirit is behind you.' I had no idea what I was looking for but I was looking for it. Whoever was speaking never gave a description other than the words 'It' or 'Spirit.' I have told people about that night and have always wished that I could have also been one to see what they told me later they saw." Maybe the reason he did not get to go was to acknowledge the fact that something was going on in the room. He was always physically present in the room. Four years later I was talking to a woman about James and I said, "I still wonder why he did not take the journey." She looked at me and said, "It is evident why James did not go. He was you three women's anchor to this World. He kept bringing you back." This woman was put in front of me to at last give me the answer, as many people had asked me that question. Why didn't James get to take the journey?

MarJoe

I am a firm believer that God gives us only what we can handle at any given time. At the time of mother's death and with all that transpired, the five and one half hours journey by Pat, Carol and myself, I'm sure that our Creator felt we had all we could take or handle for now. About four years later I was sitting in my living room and I had a flash back of the events in that bedroom as mother was dying. I remembered all going on in the room but little did I know how I was able to do this. The flash back gave me that answer. When I was asked to speak to groups about this experience I never knew why I said, 'I was standing in darkness. I could see my body from a side view as though I was looking at something in front of me. I saw my hair, my forehead, my nose, my chin, and body in darkness and everything in front of the physical body was all lit up with the whitest white I had ever seen.' Then I knew God was giving me more knowledge about that night. If I saw my physical body, it was my spirit's body looking at my physical body. I was out of my body. Whoa. What a shock! Also at one point I saw Pat completely engulf in white light from head to toe. She was sitting at the head of the bed and from the waist down legs not visible. Yet, I saw her completely engulfed in white light as, being in a cocoon. I was directly in front of her. How did I get there? My spirit had left my physical body, and left me standing motionless at the foot of the bed.

Connecting With God

Pat

I am still living in Texas. It is the evening of July 30th 1999. I had just let my dogs out in the backyard and was standing at the window watching them play with each other in the yard. I noticed that it is so very quiet inside the house. All of a sudden I began to feel things beginning to change in my head, a feeling that I had never experienced before. I felt as though my brain was being pushed, from the right to the left, inside my skull. I heard a voice say, "Get ready." Now I have never heard that voice before but I can tell you there was no doubt in my mind whose voice it was. It was God speaking to me. Sometimes the voice was in the language that I understand, English, and sometimes it was like in a foreign tongue, babbling sounding but I understood every word that was said to me. Again "Get ready. There will be a movie made from this book and my people will see just how powerful I am. If my people do not change, Jesus is coming. Tell, there will be a great revival soon."

That has been seventeen years ago and I am still waiting and telling what God told me. Now we can all wait together.

Jeremiah 20:9 But if I say I will not mention his word or speak anymore in his name "his words are in my heart like a fire consuming me, I am weary of holding it in; indeed I cannot."

Is Heaven Only For You?

Well let's start with what we know. Rev. 19: 11 "I saw heaven opened, and behold, a white horse! The one sitting on it is call Faithful and True, and in righteousness he judges and make war." Rev.19: 14 "And the armies of heaven, dressed in the finest of pure white linen, were following him on white horses." So this certainly leads us to believe that we have one species of animal in heaven.

Now who do we know that has spoken about animals in heaven? Pope II, Pope VI, and Pope Francis.

Pope John Paul II—During a public audience in 1990, the Holy Father affirmed that the animals, like men, were given the 'breath of life' by God. At the Pope's statement, Monsignor Canciani, who welcome dogs and cats into his Church in Rome, said he had experienced a great joy. When the Pope stated that 'also the animals possess a soul and that men must love and feel solidarity with our smaller brethren', I felt greatly moved. At last my work for the world of animals had been rewarded. By *Mimmo Pacifici Rome, January 1990* Translated by Piera Smith from Genre Magazine and Man/Nature/Animals, January 1990.

Pope Paul VI—Was said to have once told a distraught boy whose dog had died: "One day, we will see our animals again in the eternity of Christ. Paradise is open to all of God's creatures."

POPE Francis—It seems like he agrees; in *Laudato Si'* *(24 May 2015)* he writes that animals will join humans in the kingdom of heaven.

"Eternal life will be a shared experience of awe, in which each creature resplendently transfigured, will take its rightful place and have something to give those poor men and women who will have been liberated once and for all", the text reads.

By immortalizing his words in writing, the pope leaves no room for misunderstanding or hearsay: dogs and our other animal companions will join us in the Kingdom of Heaven.

This passage within the encyclical is short but surprisingly important and not only to catholic animal lovers everywhere. It also hints at the history of past popes' consideration for animals (which is reflected in the name he chose to bear as pope). Article by *Shanna Johnson in U.S. Catholic: Faith in real Life (February 2016)*

An age old question for many. The bible mentions in many scriptures about animals and their value to God. Deut. 5:12 "Observe the Sabbath day by keeping it holy, as the Lord your God commanded you. Six days you shall labor and do all your work but on the seventh is a Sabbath to the lord your God. On it you shall not do any work, neither you, nor your son or daughter, or your manservant or maidservant, nor your ox, your donkey, or any of your animals."

Psalm 84:3- Even the sparrow has found a home and the swallow a nest for herself, where she may have her young- a place near your altar, LORD Almighty.

Many of you have had beloved pets that have passed on; leaving you to grief and wondering if you will ever see them again.

During some of my speaking engagements there were always questions and/or stories from the audience about their animals. These are some of their stories that they shared with us.

I would ask, "What do you think about animals going to Heaven?" It sounds like you have a story to tell us.

A Woman from the Pacific Northwest

1) I was lying in my bed reading a book, as I always do before going to sleep. All of a sudden my dog that had died a year ago was laying there on my chest, looking straight into my eyes, as if to let me know that she was okay. As fast as she appeared,

she was gone. But never from my heart. It was wonderful to see her again.

A Woman from Texas

2) I was in the kitchen getting breakfast ready before my husband and I were to leave for church. He was in the bathroom shaving. I looked up and there he stood, white as a ghost. I said, "What is wrong?" He answered, "I have to tell you something, but you are never, never to tell anyone. I was shaving and heard this beautiful young male voice talking to me. 'I want to thank you two for taking such wonderful care of me those twelve 1/2 years that I was with you.' That was our little dog, that had died, talking to me. 'And by the way they will be singing the Alleluia chorus today' said the voice. Sure enough that was the hymn sung at church. But as far as never telling anyone, I will tell this story to anyone that will listen to me.

A Gentleman from Dallas, Texas

3) I live in Dallas and if you know anything about its weather. Especially, the thunderstorms it can be quite scary. Across the sky, lightening, pouring down rain and heavy winds. When this happens my four small dogs will run and usually hide under the bed. On this particular day the storm came in but I noticed my four dogs were on their hind legs looking out window. I walked over to the window and looked outside. I then walked to the door and opened it, the four dogs ran outside into rain and lightening exploding across the sky. I watched, with tears in my eyes, the dogs running and playing with their beloved, McGregor, my dog, their friend and pal, that had passed away a year ago.

My Personal Experiences

4) I was driving home to Marblemount when I started through Rockport State Park on highway 20. There lying on the right side of the road I spotted a dead deer that had been hit by a car. I said to myself, 'You poor little thing, you didn't make it across.' About 200 feet up the road my car beams shown straight through this huge beautiful deer and light around it. Then I said, 'You did make it to the other side.' Then I realized I had not said to the other side of the road. God let me know, in that moment, that the deer in its magnificent body had indeed made it to the Other Side.

5) I was taking care of a woman who was confined to her bed. She had a little dog that gave her great pleasure and comfort, and stayed in her room with her the majority of the time. I was getting ready to get dinner started and glanced over toward the living room, as I headed to the kitchen. I saw a medium size black dog, walking between the couch and coffee table, and as it walked toward the window it disappeared. I went into the bedroom and asked her if she ever had another dog besides Jiggles. I asked her what color was it and how big. Her description matched that of the dog that I had just seen. I told her, "Well I just saw that dog in the living room, and then it vanished." She replied, "This house talks to you doesn't it." Then she looked over at me and smiled.

Rainbow Bridge

Just this side of Heaven is a place called Rainbow Bridge.

When an animal dies that has been especially close to someone here, that pet goes to Rainbow Bridge.

There are meadows and hills for all of our special friends so they can run and play together.

There is plenty of food, water and sunshine, and our friends are warm and comfortable.

All the animals who had been ill and old are restored to health and vigor; those who were hurt or maimed are made whole and strong again, just as we remember them in our dreams of days and times gone by.

The animals are happy and content, except for one small thing; they each miss someone very special to them, who had to be left behind.

They all run and play together, but the day comes when one suddenly stops and looks into the distance. His bright eyes are intent; His eager body quivers. Suddenly he begins to run from the group, flying over the green grass, his legs carrying him faster and faster.

You have been spotted, and when you and your special friend finally meet, you cling together in joyous reunion, never to be parted again. The happy kisses rain upon your face; your hands again caress the beloved head, and you look once more into the trusting eyes of your pet, so long gone from your life but never absent from your heart.

Then you cross Rainbow Bridge together....

Author unknown...

Our beloved Brandy

"Our final resting place." Liberty Bell Mountain Washington Pass N. Cascade mountains.